LANGUAGE &
THE PURSUIT OF
TRUTH

JOHN WILSON

LANGUAGE & THE PURSUIT OF TRUTH

CAMBRIDGE UNIVERSITY PRESS

Published by the Syndics of the Cambridge University Press
Bentley House, 200 Euston Road, London NW1 2DB
American Branch: 32 East 57th Street, New York, N.Y.10022

ISBN: 0 521 09421 6

First published 1956
Reprinted 1958, 1960, 1967
First paperback edition 1967
Reprinted 1969, 1974

First printed in Great Britain at the Stellar Press,
Union Street, Barnet, Herts
Reprinted in Great Britain by
Hazell Watson & Viney Ltd, Aylesbury, Bucks

CONTENTS

Chapter III. TRUTH

PREFACE

THIS book is an attempt to do something new: to present semantics, which is the study of linguistic communication, to the general public. Since it is new, therefore, I must spend some time explaining what this study involves and why it is important enough to merit the attention which it has so far escaped.

The study of linguistic communication involves a great deal more than a knowledge of the grammar, syntax, style, literature or etymology of any language or languages. It attempts to improve our rational understanding of language in general, and our ability to argue, to answer questions, and to solve problems through the medium of words. It has been found impossible to do this effectively without regard to basic considerations, including the meanings of words and statements, their logical classification, and their various methods of verification. Although a knowledge of grammar and of the usage of one or more languages plainly ministers to this end, it would be idle to maintain that such knowledge was adequate to satisfy it completely.

Yet it does not take long to see how important the end is, and how important it is that we should take serious notice of any means which might help to bring it about. This importance is immensely increased by prevailing international conditions. All disputes and disagreements between nations must be conducted, either by blows, or by words: either by compulsion, or by persuasion: either by violence, or by peaceful discussion. The effects of modern tyranny and modern war are probably worse, and certainly more horrifying, than those of any past age; yet the number and intensity of our disputes do not seem to have decreased. The exchange of force seems not only unpleasant, but ineffective as a method of solving problems. The exchange of argument is our only possible substitute; and since our arguments are necessarily expressed in language, the importance of the study of communication is enormous. The necessity of 'understanding our neighbours' inevitably entails understanding what our neighbours say and mean, and having the mental equipment necessary for assessing the value of their views. We live in a world where most nations, through ignorance as well as through innate hostility, are both unable and unwilling to understand each other. They use words as slogans or banners, stopping but rarely to understand or evaluate their meaning and truth. It is evident, for example, that the words 'democracy' and 'freedom' mean different things to the Western world and to Soviet Russia: yet neither side ever discusses these ideals on a linguistic basis. On such fundamental issues, communication is at its worst where it is most needed. When such conditions prevail, it becomes the duty of all those who desire peace and co-operation amongst the nations to acquire the ability to handle and understand language properly.

Within a democratic state, this duty should be even more obvious to each individual citizen. For each citizen has the power, either to add to our understanding or to add to our misunderstanding of the problems which face us; the advantages of a good system of communication, and the dangers of a bad one, are both enormously increased. We can all either contribute to our common store of facts and our logical use of them, or swell the falsehoods and the irrational appeal of propaganda, advertisement and demagogy. All the most important problems, the problems of religion, morals, politics, and sociology, can only be solved via the use of words. To understand the use of words properly is plainly a prior condition of solving them successfully.

This argument might be put even more strongly. It is sufficiently obvious to the most amateur students of language that the discovery of truth and the attainment of knowledge necessarily depend on a good understanding of language: in particular, of the notions of meaning and verification. This vital point has not really been grasped at all: yet until it is grasped, we cannot hope to make progress in our views on moral, political and religious questions. At present we are confined to restating our beliefs merely, in various forms of words which we ourselves only partly understand, and whose truth we have no notion how to prove. I have made this point at greater length in chapters III and IV. Here it will be enough to say that insofar as our education is intended to help children and adults to know the truth on matters of moral, political and religious importance, it must use the study of language as one of its most important methods, if it is to be of any value at all.

Many more arguments besides these could be brought forward: some, even, which might be thought more cogent. I could point to the importance of linguistic understanding in personal relationships, and quote that most just observation, 'All tragedy is the failure of communication'. I could argue from a non-utilitarian standpoint, and claim that the study of man's supreme form of rational expression, and the feature which most clearly distinguishes him from the lower animals, is one of the fittest and most noble that the human mind could pursue: that its usefulness is as great (though more often taken for granted) as the usefulness of many other studies to which we have long devoted a great deal of our time and energy: that there are few of man's abilities which are more worthy of our understanding than his linguistic ability, which has brought him not only his power, but also his knowledge, his poetry, and the opportunity to frame his ideals.

Many people might agree that the teaching of semantics is desirable, but at the same time believe it to be impracticable. My own experience at least does not support this view: I have met with more success and interest in teaching it than in teaching any other subject. There is plenty of evidence to show that this experience need not be exceptional: for the subject does not require an unusual intelligence. It requires only the patience to master a particular technique: a requirement shared by most other important subjects. As to the difficulty of putting the subject across clearly—this book itself will have to stand as an answer to that charge.

I would claim, indeed, that the study of language fills a need which is at least half-consciously felt by many people. Most men seek enlightenment on the more general issues of morals, politics and religion (to name but a few fields of study). Semantics offers a basic discipline of thought on all such matters: a discipline which saves a great deal of time in the long run. It is easy to air one's views in a vague and uncritical manner: not so easy, but far more valuable, to produce an objective analysis and constructive argument. The difficulties we experience in trying to do the latter are not due simply to strictly logical fallacies, or to the use of tendentious or irrelevant verbiage: they arise from a basic failure to understand the nature and the logic of language itself. It is not a question merely of exercising intelligence and will-power: it is a question of mastering a science and a mental discipline.

I have tried to write so as to be well within the range of comprehension of the non-specialist reader; I have omitted formal and symbolic logic, which are unnecessary for my purpose; and I have reduced the number of necessary technical terms to a minimum. In view of the novelty of the subject, however, I should like to warn the reader against taking the various sections of the book too quickly. A thorough understanding of each is essential.

ACKNOWLEDGEMENTS

My thanks are due to the teaching of Professor H. L. A. Hart and Mr Stuart Hampshire, and particularly to Professor R. B. Braithwaite for his kindness in offering so many invaluable suggestions.

J.W.

SELECT BIBLIOGRAPHY

This bibliography is intended only to provide a list of some few books which students will find useful for further reading. Those who are unacquainted with modern philosophical literature will find that those in the first group make easier reading than those in the second.

STUART CHASE, *The Tyranny of Words*.
GEORGE ORWELL, *1984*.
JOHN WILSON, *Thinking with Concepts*.
L. S. STEBBING, *Thinking to some Purpose*.
R. H. THOULESS, *Straight and Crooked Thinking*.

ALASDAIR MACINTYRE, *A Short History of Ethics*.
JOHN WILSON, *Reason and Morals*.
A. J. AYER, *Language, Truth and Logic*.
P. H. NOWELL-SMITH, *Ethics*.
G. RYLE, *The Concept of Mind*.
C. K. OGDEN and I. A. RICHARDS, *The Meaning of Meaning*.
J. L. AUSTIN, *How to Do Things with Words*.

CHAPTER I

WORDS

A. THE FUNCTION OF WORDS

WORDS are tools, which only human beings can use intelligently. The advantages of being able to use such tools are obvious enough; the advantages of being able to use them with the efficiency that comes from true understanding will, I hope, become equally obvious as we proceed. What we are considering now is the way in which words give us these advantages, or how the tools manage to do their job.

We use words with one general purpose in view: so that other people shall understand us. Words enable us to achieve this purpose for one all-important reason. *They act as signs*. A sign is something which conveys meaning and can be interpreted. Some signs are natural, and not artificial or man-made; thus, for example, we say that dark clouds are a sign of rain, meaning that we know from the dark clouds that rain is coming. But when we communicate with each other, and understand each other, we make use of artificial signs, signs which we have invented for the specific purpose of making ourselves understood.

The importance of studying and improving our use of these artificial signs is immense, for it is virtually impossible to advance our knowledge and our understanding of various problems without using a good system of signs, and using it properly. The history of mathematics shows this very clearly. The development of a good system of notation made it possible to take great strides in our mathematical knowledge, which the Romans could never have made. Try multiplying XCIX by XXXIV, and see how hard it is.

Not all artificial signs are words. Here are some others:

1. Gestures: e.g. pointing to something to draw attention to it, shrugging your shoulders to show that you don't know or care about something, shaking your fist to show anger and defiance.

2. Special codes: e.g. semaphore (a highly-developed form of gestures), the Morse code, cipher codes and so on.

3. Written signs: e.g. arrows directing your attention, the 30 m.p.h. limit sign, and the signs of arithmetic and algebra (plus, minus, equals, etc.).

4. Colour- and picture-signs: e.g. a red stop-light, road signs like 'hump-back bridge', 'steep hill' and 'road narrows'.

5. Sound-signs: e.g. a bell ringing for school, or a gong for dinner.

There is nothing common to all these in themselves: what is common to them is the fact that people have agreed to use them in certain recognised ways. Because of this agreement, they convey the same information to everyone. There is no particular reason why a red light should mean 'stop' or 'danger', and a green light 'go' or 'safety': it is simply that we have chosen these signs to do this particular job. If we could get used to it, they would work perfectly well the other way round.

We can now see that almost anything can be successfully used as a sign, provided we agree about what its use is to be. It is our agreement about its use, and not the sign itself, which enables us to communicate. From this a very important conclusion follows: that signs do not have meaning in themselves, but only in relation to our agreement about their use. Thus in England a red light means 'stop'; but in another country it might mean 'go'. It would be absurd to ask what the 'real' meaning was. One country is not wrong, and the other right: it is not a question of being right or wrong at all. To say that a red light means 'stop' in England is just to say that the English have agreed that a red light is to act as a sign for behaving in a certain way, namely stopping. In another country they might have agreed to make it act as a sign for going.

That is why I began by saying that words are tools. For words are simply signs, and signs are like tools because we use them to do certain jobs. All people who speak the same language have agreed to use certain words for certain jobs and this enables them to communicate with each other. There is nothing particularly remarkable about the words themselves: they might just as well have chosen different ones. What matters is that this agreement about the use of words should be fully understood, and understood in detail, by everyone who wishes to profit from it. Let us go back for a minute to the use of non-verbal signs, and take the example of bell-ringing. By itself, the ringing of a bell means nothing. But in certain recognised contexts, it may mean things as different as 'time for school!', 'somebody at the door!', 'come to church!', 'that's the end of the lesson', or 'come here please, waitress!' We might well wonder how it is that the same noise can mean so many different things; but of course the answer is easy. The noise occurs in recognised contexts: in times and places and circumstances when we know that it can only mean one thing.

Thus not only can almost anything be used as a sign, but almost any sign can be used to communicate several different things. Everything depends on our agreement about, and our understanding of, the ways in which we use signs. Let us apply this to verbal signs, or words. First, any convenient collection of letters can be used as a word. We can communicate just as well by using 'father', 'pater', 'Vater', 'père', 'Daddy', 'Pop', or anything else: provided we are understood, it makes no difference. We could even invent a completely new word, or decide to spell and pronounce one of the old words backwards. Secondly, the same collection of letters can be used to communicate quite different things. The word 'port' can mean a special sort of wine, the opposite of starboard, a harbour, and various other things: the word 'bat' can mean either the sort of thing you play cricket with, or the sort of thing you find in belfries.

The significance of any sign, therefore, depends on the context in which it is used. Sometimes the context is supplied by what the speaker is doing, or what tone of voice he uses. Thus when a child says simply 'Ball', he may mean 'Look at that ball', or 'Give me my ball', or even 'Take the beastly ball away!' We can often tell which he means by the way in which he says it. But an adult, who has learnt to speak any language well, does not need to rely upon tone of voice or gestures. For a language is an immensely complex system of signs which depend on each other for their significance. The adult knows the rules which govern this system, and can thus give the signs their proper significance by using them in their proper contexts. The child can only handle the sign 'ball': the adult can handle other signs, like 'look at', 'give', 'the', and 'take away'. What the adult does by his knowledge of how to use these signs, the child tries to do by gesture and tone of voice.

We can see, then, that the ability to use a language

depends on more than a simple agreement about what each individual sign is supposed to communicate. We have also to agree about how to use various signs in conjunction with each other. This is why, if we want to learn how to use a language properly, it is helpful to learn the rules of its grammar and syntax. These represent the structure of the language, and show us the right ways of putting its individual words together. Without agreement on these ways our communication would not get very far. For example: we might agree on the use of the individual sign 'train', and the individual sign 'come'. We could then use short sentences like 'Train come'. This would be quite useful: but consider how invaluable it would be to agree also about the use of words like 'has', 'will', 'not', 'if', and so on. Then we could use sentences like 'Train has come', 'Train will not come', etc. We could go further, and agree about the use of words like 'a' and 'the', and about the proper word-order to use for a question; then we could say 'The train will come', or 'Will the train come?' With a great deal more agreement, we might eventually be able to communicate by means of complex sentences like 'I am afraid that, if the train has not come, it will never come'.

In a fully-developed language, therefore, communication is a much more complex matter. It is not just a question of having different signs or signals, like bells ringing or red lights flashing, each of which 'stands for' a different 'thing'. Indeed, it now seems that it is misleading to talk of words 'standing for things', or 'having meanings'. They only have *uses*; and these uses are largely determined by the rules of the language. 'The train will come' and 'Will the train come?' do not communicate the same 'thing' at all: and yet the same words are used. It is their order which makes the difference; and order is only one of the relationships which may exist between words. Learning to communicate by means of a language is rather like learning to play a game. We have to learn the rules and the purposes of the rules, and how the various parts of the game are related. Only by learning these can we play the game successfully. In just the same way, successful communication depends on our understanding of the language-rules which govern the use of words.

B. TYPES OF WORDS

If we realise the full implication of the way in which words function as signs, we shall also realise that it would be unprofitable to investigate the functions of different types of words in themselves; for everything depends, not on the words themselves, but on the way in which we use them. In considering different types of words, therefore, we must ask the right sort of questions. A question like 'What does so-and-so stand for?' or 'What is such-and-such a sign of?' is likely to mislead us. For such questions take it for granted that for each sign or word there is a 'thing' in the world outside to which the sign or word corresponds. This suggests that the outside world is neatly parcelled up into 'things', and all we have to do is to learn to put the right verbal labels on them. Thus there is supposed to be one 'thing' to which we attach the label 'elephant', and various 'things' which we call 'properties' or 'qualities' of the elephant, and label 'huge', 'grey', 'wild', and so forth.

Unfortunately it is not so easy as this. First, it is not true that we find the world parcelled up for us into 'things'. It is we who do the parcelling. When we are first born into this world, we do not immediately perceive objects and qualities: all that we experience is a glorious muddle of sounds, colours, tastes, smells, and other phenomena which reach us through our senses. We have no idea of seeing in perspective, and we cannot distinguish one object from another. We have to learn to put our experience in order, to group our sense-impressions into a satisfactory pattern. There is nothing logically necessary in the way in which we group them: we simply happen to find that some ways are convenient. One of the most convenient ways is to separate the world out into 'things' and 'qualities': and this way of treating the world is reflected in our language. Indeed, our language and our setting in order of our experience are closely interrelated, and influence each other. But we must remember that though this language is a natural growth, and a most useful tool, it is not logically inevitable, and may not suffice for all purposes.

Secondly, it is plain that a great many words do not 'stand for' anything at all, and that most signs are not signs *of* any special 'thing' in the world. Concrete nouns like 'elephant', and adjectives like 'huge', 'wild', 'blue' and so forth do look like labels for 'things'; but few other words can be explained in this way. 'Symmetry', 'liberty', 'humanity' and 'squareness' do not stand for things: nor do 'equal', 'unfortunate', 'good', and 'negative'. When we turn to the other parts of speech, the fact is even more obvious: 'kill', 'quickly', 'Alas!', 'this', 'under', and 'if' do not even look as if they stood for things.

Why, then, are we misled in this fashion? Chiefly because we have a strong and almost unescapable prejudice in favour of *naming* the various experiences which we have from childhood onwards. We feel that to bestow names on things is somehow to control them, or at any rate to feel familiar with them. We find, as children, that the word

'Mama' or 'Dadda' increases our power over our environment: by calling these names we can summon either one of our parents to attend to us. Consequently, we have a strong bias in favour of treating all nouns and adjectives at least as if they were proper names: as if there was one single object to which they could be attached. We assume that when we say 'justice' or 'humanity' we are naming something, just as we are naming something when we say 'John Smith' or 'Judas Iscariot'.

But our actual use of signs is more complicated than that. Only proper nouns name things. Not even nouns like 'elephant' name things. There is this elephant, and that elephant, and the other elephant, but there is no single thing 'elephant'. 'Elephant' is a class-noun. We cannot say what it names, because it does not name anything. All we can say is that it can be correctly used in certain circumstances, that it is a noun, and that it has to be used in accordance with certain grammatical and syntactical rules. Nor do adjectives name things. There is no single thing 'hugeness' which we observe in elephants, whales, battleships, giants and so forth. Still less are there 'things' like symmetry, or misfortune, or visibility. The more abstract and removed from our sense-experience the nouns and adjectives we use, the more absurd does the theory appear. It all stems from our love of proper names.

The true explanation for our ability to use one word in many contexts is that, although we do not perceive 'things' and then invent one label for each 'thing', we do perceive similarities in our experience. We observe that certain features of our experience keep cropping up, that certain experiences are recurrent. If the same experience recurs often enough to make it worth our while, we invent a word or sign to use on any occasion when we wish to communicate the experience. We see that pillar-boxes, poppies, and stop-lights are similar in one respect: and so we use the word 'red' to express this similarity. We perceive that certain things are similar in many respects: say, they are all small, circular, and hard; and we invent a noun for the occasions when we wish to speak of any of these things, the noun 'penny'. We observe the penny doing something on various occasions, which we afterwards call 'rolling'. We see it rolling in certain recurrent ways, which we call 'quickly' or 'slowly'. In this way we build up a vocabulary of nouns, adjectives, verbs and adverbs. All of them bear some relation to our experience, but none of them except proper nouns name things.

A much more profitable way of considering the different functions of different types of words, then, is to consider their use; and we have already seen the use of some sorts of nouns, verbs, adjectives and adverbs. They act as a kind of shorthand, giving us a number of signs which we can use whenever appropriate. This shorthand is essential for communication, for we could not possibly have one sign for every part of our experience which we wish to speak about. It is because of the recurrent similarities in experience that the shorthand is possible. But the majority of words have uses quite different to these.

Prepositions like 'in' and 'under' are used when we want to talk about the relations between parts of our experience, and cannot be used except to specify something about nouns or pronouns. This use also depends on similarities in our experience: there are many cases of something being in something else, or under something else. But here we are obviously beginning to move further away from our direct experience. We feel no temptation to say that 'in' or 'under' mean something in themselves: on the contrary, their meaning is determined by their context. Even more so in the case of pronouns: 'this', 'that', 'he', 'it', 'some' and 'other' are not words which refer directly to any experience, still less to any single experience. Only their context can tell us what is being referred to. These words obey grammatical rules, and can only be used in certain circumstances: but they do not stand for things. Interjections like 'Good heavens!' are meaningless without their contexts. We feel inclined to say that such phrases *mean* nothing: they simply *express* surprise, grief, joy, and so forth. Finally, conjunctions and articles ('if', 'therefore', 'and', 'the') can obviously be dealt with only by observing their use within sentences and clauses, not by trying to tie them down to experience.

We can only classify different types of words, therefore, by first considering what it is that we are trying to do when we use language, and of course we are often trying to do very different things. We shall consider what these are more fully in the next chapter, when we look at the uses of complexes of signs, or statements. Nevertheless, we can distinguish certain types of single words which have a fairly constant function, and since these words play an important part in our statements it will be as well to consider them immediately.

The demands which we make upon our language are almost infinite, and no two words fulfil quite the same purpose in communication. The following list of word-types cannot be considered exhaustive; but it will give us some idea of the basic uses to which we put our verbal signs.

1. Descriptive words

One of the most fundamental uses to which words can

be put is to describe our experience. By 'describing our experience' I mean giving some sort of information about the world outside. Sentences like 'The cat is on the mat', and 'All swans are white', attempt to give such information. Describing experience involves the use of many different parts of speech, but in particular of nouns, adjectives, verbs, adverbs, and prepositions. These form the basis of our descriptions, though we add to them by using words which have different functions.

Some descriptive words are simple and concrete, like 'elephant', 'grey' and 'walking': others are further removed from our direct sense-experience, like 'symmetry', 'coordination', and 'unite'. A great many nouns are a long way distant from our immediate experience. Abstract nouns like 'Christianity' summarise a great many of our experiences in a convenient form: 'Christianity' means 'the beliefs and practices of Christians', and 'the beliefs of practices of Christians' is itself only a short way of expressing all the many and varied beliefs and practices, which we should otherwise have to enumerate in full.

We must remember that what we wish to describe, and the things about which we wish to give information, may be of very different kinds. We may wish to call attention to one particular fact, in which case we shall probably use simple nouns and verbs, as in the sentence 'William the Conqueror won the Battle of Hastings in 1066'. Or we may wish to convey information of a wider and more complex nature, as in the sentence 'The Norman way of life began to establish itself in England in 1066'. The more we want to generalise, the more ground we shall have to cover, and the more abstract and removed from particular experience will be our descriptive words. A fair test of how abstracted a descriptive word is can be conducted by seeing how easy it is to form a mental image of what the word describes. Thus we can form a good image of 'a cat': but it is more difficult to form an image of 'felines' or 'creatures', and practically impossible to form one of 'life' or 'nature'.

Different kinds of descriptive words do different jobs: and the variety of these jobs is enormous. Some words, like 'intelligent' or 'fragile' describe the tendencies of people or things to behave in certain ways: in these examples, to solve problems competently, and to break easily. Others, like 'equal' or 'unlike' describe relations between things. Others again, like 'negative' or 'significant' describe the uses and functions of words. Everything depends on what it is that we wish to describe.

The words by which we express scientific concepts, for instance, are descriptive in a peculiar way. When we speak of 'an electron', we are not talking of something which we experience directly, as we experience a billiard-ball. We can see billiard-balls, but we cannot see electrons: all we can see is the way in which our measuring instruments behave under certain circumstances. So too with 'gravity'. We can observe bodies being attracted to each other, but apart from this we have no direct observation of a particular force called gravity. Gravity and electrons are not things in the same sense that billiard-balls and falling bodies are things. The words are used to express concepts; and their meaning is partly determined by our observations and experience, but partly also by the role which they play in scientific theory. Thus in mechanics words like 'work', 'mass', and 'force' are used on a far more abstract level than they are used in non-scientific contexts; and though their meaning can always be explained in terms of experience, it is also determined by their technical use within the science of mechanics. The definitions of such words given in scientific text-books are those which scientists have found most useful to adopt. They are descriptive words, in our broad sense of 'descriptive', but it must also be remembered that they are technical terms.

From these examples it will be seen that the status of descriptive words is not always obvious. Many such words, like the words of science, are not used simply to describe our direct observations or immediate experience. They are abstractions: and abstractions may be made, not only at different levels, but for difference purposes. A biologist, for instance, might classify animals in several different ways, none of which might seem to the layman to bear very much relation to what he himself could observe about the animals. This is simply because different types of classification serve different purposes. Thus, you could classify them in one way if you were interested in the history of their evolution, in another way if you were interested in how they got their food, in a third way if you were interested in how they produced their young, and so on. With descriptive words, then, we must remember that their meaning depends on what it is that we wish to describe, and what our purposes are when we use them.

2. *Evaluative words*

By 'evaluative words' I mean words which we use when we want to do more than just describe things: words which we use to praise, blame, commend or criticise. Such words give or deny value to the things or people they are applied to: they 'evaluate'. When I say of something or someone that it or he is 'good', for instance, I am commending or praising: when I say that it is 'bad' or 'evil' I am criticising or deprecating it. In the first case I am saying that it is the sort of thing which you ought to choose, in the second that it is the sort of thing which you ought not to choose.

There are very few words which are only evaluative, in the sense that they give us no information at all about what is being evaluated. Most words are a mixture of evaluative and descriptive: that is, they not only tell us something about a person or thing, but also commend or deprecate it. Words like 'steal' and 'murder' are mixtures. 'Steal' means partly 'to take property that legally belongs to another': this is its descriptive meaning. But it also means 'when it is wrong to do so': and this is evaluative. 'Murder' means 'killing when it is wrong to do so', a similar mixture. Hence judges and soldiers are not said to 'murder', because it is believed that condemning a man to death in the law-court and killing men on the field of battle are not wrong: hence it is not sense to call these actions 'murder', although they are both killing.

A few simple words like 'good', 'ought' and 'right' are almost purely evaluative, though they may acquire descriptive meaning in certain contexts. A farmer and a jockey can both speak of a 'good' horse. Insofar as they are describing the horse, they both mean different things. The farmer will probably mean a sturdy, well-built horse, which can pull his plough efficiently: the jockey, a lithe, fast horse, which can win the Derby. But insofar as they are evaluating or commending the horse, they both mean the same. The fact that they both use the word 'good' does not by itself tell you anything about the horse: it tells you only that they wish to commend it.

Such words are rare, however, and are usually employed when the context of their use is clear. When the farmer speaks of a 'good' horse, I can guess what sort of horse it is, because I know what sort of horses farmers wish to commend. If I did not know, I would have no idea what sort of horse he meant when he called it 'good'. In other words, 'good' can be used to commend anything or anybody: it does not tie us down to any special descriptive meaning, unless we use it in a recognised context. It would be odd to say that coal was 'good' coal if it did not burn properly in any sort of fire: but this is because we all commend coal for the same reasons, and use the same principles of judgment or criteria in evaluating coal. But it would not be absurd, because we might just possibly be considering the coal from another point of view: perhaps we want to use it to throw at people, or perhaps we are artists and want to paint it. In that case we shall be interested, not in its ability to burn well, but in quite different things about it: and in virtue of these things we might quite well call it 'good'. The word implies that we have in our minds certain criteria or principles of judgment in reference to which we wish to commend it, but we are not logically compelled to have in mind any particular set of criteria. The word can be applied to anything on any criteria, provided we have *some* criteria: it is like a blank cheque which we can fill in with anybody's name, provided we have reason for paying him money.

The majority of words do not have this wide use, and are tied down to a particular descriptive meaning. I have already quoted 'steal' and 'murder' as examples. Consider also the words 'merciful' and 'just'. Both these are words of commendation: we have a favourable or approving attitude towards merciful or just actions. But apart from this, the two words do not describe the same sort of action at all. A just action is one which carries out the principle of retribution—repaying good with good, and evil with evil, or rewarding virtue and punishing vice. Merciful

27

actions, on the other hand, often go against this principle. When a jury 'recommends mercy', it is suggesting that we overlook retributive justice in a particular case.

It is also possible for two words to have the same descriptive meaning, and yet to have different evaluative meanings. One person might maintain that Scott's attempt to reach the Pole, or Hillary's climbing of Everest, was 'courageous': another might call it 'rash' or 'foolhardy'. They might both be in complete agreement about the facts of the matter: both would admit that Scott and Hillary were good at facing danger, and that they undertook to suffer perils which other men would refuse to suffer. In other words, they would agree about all that can be *described* about their actions. But they would place different values upon them. The first would hold that it was right for them to undergo the dangers, the second that it was wrong. Hence they both use the word which expresses their evaluation of these attempts. The first calls them 'courageous': the second, 'rash'.

3. Pointer words

These are words which have vitally important logical functions within phrases and sentences, but which do not describe or commend. Successful communication depends largely on their correct use: for this use does a great deal to make *sense* of our communication. Most, but not all, of them are pronouns and conjunctions: and we must include also the articles 'a' and 'the'. All these words are 'pointers' in that they point out to us the sense of any sentence or phrase.

A great many pronouns are pointers in the literal sense that they are used in place of the gesture of pointing to something. This enables us to understand what is being referred to. If I say 'This typewriter is a good one', the

word 'this' shows the person I am talking to what typewriter I am talking about. 'This' points at something
near me. 'That', on the other hand, points at something
which is some distance away. 'I' points at myself, or rather
at the person who uses it: 'you' at the person spoken to:
'he' at a third person. 'Here' and 'now' both perform the
same kind of function.

Other pronouns point to the sense of what we are saying
in a less obvious way. Words like 'all', 'some', 'himself',
'neither' and 'whoever' add logical qualifications to what
we are saying. They qualify descriptions, but do not themselves describe. Thus there is a great difference between
saying 'all swans' and 'some swans' and 'no swans': but
the only descriptive word used is the word 'swans'. 'All',
'some', and 'no' tell us how to understand the word
'swans': they assign to the word the part it is to play in the
sense of the sentence.

Conjunctions have only this logical function, and their
use as pointers to sense is enormous. Words like 'because',
'therefore', 'if', 'since' and 'although' are essential if we
are to carry out any communication above a primitive
level, because all reasoning and sustained thinking depends
upon them. Consider the sentences: 'Since all flies seem to
die in the wintertime, then either they leave eggs behind
them, or else they do not really all die, because there are
always plenty of flies next summer. They do not leave eggs
behind them: therefore they do not really all die.' Now try
to express this reasoning without using conjunctions and
other logical words like 'since', 'all', 'then, 'either',
'because' and so on. It would be impossible. Logical words
are good guides to logical thinking and speaking, and
an incorrect use of them nearly always indicates bad
reasoning.

4. *Interjections*

There is no special difficulty about the function of ex-
clamations, which is simply to express our feelings, and not
to convey logical sense at all. If I say 'Good heavens!' I
am not actually referring to something in my experience,
namely the heavens, and commending them: I am simply
uttering an exclamation, and do not expect to be taken
literally. They are significant, however, in that their use
tends to intrude upon the use of other words. If on going
into battle I shout 'St George for merry England!', it is
not at all clear whether I am making a statement ('Let us
remember our patron saint, and fight well for merry
England'), or simply uttering a virtually meaningless war-
cry. In certain cases we can confidently assert that nothing
is meant literally at all. The word 'Blimey', for instance,
which is a corruption of 'Blind me!', is obviously only used
as an oath, not as a command. But many other cases are
on the borderline. It is probable that when the French
mob during the Revolution shouted 'Down with the
aristocrats!', they meant precisely what they said; no
doubt they were expressing their feelings, but they did so
in an intelligible manner, so that the hearer could understand exactly what they felt about what. On the other
hand, when after a public performance of some kind in
this country we sing 'God save the Queen', it is doubtful
whether we are really using these words to communicate
anything certain or definite. The more thoughtful or
patriotic of us may certainly do so, but in most cases we
would be inclined to say that the words are used rather as
ritual is used: not to communicate anything certain, but
to express our feelings or our regard for good form and
convention.

From these examples we can see that it is a mistake to

suppose that all our words and sentences are to be taken as deliberate and meaningful pieces of communication. Interjections often appear to take the form of descriptive or other words. We must not judge by the appearance or outward form of what is said, but rather by the use to which it is put; and if we consider these uses honestly, we shall find that many of our words are used as slogans, as ritual, or as merely expressive sounds.

Before leaving these different word-types, we must stress the fact that no trust can be placed in trying to find the meaning or use of any word by its grammatical classification. Nouns do not mean one sort of thing, verbs another, adjectives another, and so forth. Many of our misunderstandings are caused by adopting this view. The English language is especially deceptive in this way, because it allows us to express the same sense in a dozen different ways. If we take one way of expressing something too seriously, and pay too much attention to its grammatical form and too little to its use, we land ourselves in serious trouble. The verb 'is', for instance, fulfils so many different functions that it seems hardly worth while noticing that it is a verb. In the sentences 'It is raining', 'Religion is the opium of the people', 'There is no such thing as a unicorn', 'A puppy is a young dog', 'He is going for a walk', the word has a different meaning in each of its uses. If you take the view that verbs stand for processes or doing things, it is impossible to account for all these uses. 'Is', like many other verbs, does a unique series of jobs.

We can see how little account is to be taken of the importance of the parts of speech in understanding the sense of any communication from the following sentences, all of which mean the same but use different forms:

1. Solomon's thoughts were very wise.
2. The wisdom of Solomon's thoughts was great.
3. Solomon thought very wisely.

Our ability to play around with the nouns, verbs, adjectives and adverbs used in these sentences should make us suspicious of thinking that any part of speech can be pinned down to a particular meaning.

C. MISTAKES ABOUT WORDS

Most of our failures in communication which are caused by the abuse of single words rather than the abuse of statements result from our basic inability to distinguish the proper uses of language, and to employ the distinctions effectively. We must continually ask ourselves the question 'What am I trying to do with these words? For what purpose am I using them? And is any of them out of place?' Because we do not ask and answer these questions often enough, we fall victims to two perpetual temptations, which we must consider in turn.

1. Magic

It may seem strange in the twentieth century to suggest that we often seem to use words as if they had some sort of magical power, but this is only because we rarely stop to think what we are saying. Undoubtedly words can be used as a form of magic, as when the magician says 'Abracadabra', but it is essential to know when we are doing this, and when we are using them meaningfully in order to communicate.

Many native tribes are quite honest about the magic of words, as they see it. According to their beliefs, it is dangerous to allow an enemy to know your name, because this knowledge will give him power to kill you in some way. Many religions, also, keep the name of the god they worship a strict secret; we may even suspect that the commandment that we should not 'take the name of God in vain' arises partly from a magical use of words. The importance of knowledge of the proper names in invoking the various devils and supernatural powers of witchcraft is well known. In nearly all ancient religions (and perhaps in some modern ones also) the repetition of a form of words, without regard for their meaning, was supposed to be efficacious in curing both bodily and spiritual ills.

The same beliefs persist today. Blasphemy, which consists of using certain words (particularly names, which have a specially magic force) in a manner supposed to be improper or dangerous, is still a crime. Obscene words are still banned both by law and by convention, as if they had some sort of magical power which defiled the speaker and the hearer of the word, and corrupted the minds of people in general. Perhaps the most interesting example of this comes from the last century, when what we now call 'trousers' were not supposed to be mentioned. Unfortunately the practical usefulness of referring to the garments was too great to be overcome. Yet the taboo against the word 'trousers' still held. What happened was that the word was replaced by the word 'unmentionables', which had precisely the same meaning. This sort of taboo still exists in a rather lessened form today. It is still injudicious and impolite, when in certain circles, to refer directly to articles of ladies' underclothing by their standard names.

The taboo on 'obscene' words gives us a clue to our weakness for magic in words. We tend to regard those words as magical which refer to things that have a great emotional appeal to us, or that are regarded as private and sacred in some special way. Hence, most unmentionable words are either religious or sexual. (The importance to men of religion and sex need not be stressed here.) Consequently, it is taboo to refer to matters too directly concerned with religion or sex. In England today, when the emotional feeling about religion is not what it was a century ago, the taboo on religious words is on the decline: but the taboo on sexual words is still very strong.

Nevertheless, the taboo allows us (as in the case of 'trousers') to refer indirectly or discreetly to such matters, in so far as it is strictly necessary for some practical purpose. Thus we may speak, in a rather half-hearted way of which Othello would probably have disapproved, of a man's 'embracing' or (in progressive circles) 'sleeping with' a woman: but we must not use other more straightforward words with the same meaning. The fact that the meaning is the same in both cases shows clearly that it is the supposed magical content in the taboo-words, not their meaning, which makes them taboo.

A ritualistic form of words, where the meaning is of secondary importance, is still practised by a great many people. These rituals are supposed to have magical force; as we can see, not only from the devout way in which they are spoken, but from the more convincing fact that few of the people who speak them seem to have any idea what they mean. The use of Latin in the churches of the Middle Ages, a tongue not understood by the congregations, is a good example. The repetition by Communists of the words of Marx or Lenin, and by Fascists of the words of Hitler, is the purest ritualistic magic. Even the most ardent sceptics, and those who pride themselves on freedom from superstition, are not immune. We all use forms of words as if they had power on their own account, instead of merely being useful signs. The words 'I promise', for instance, whose proper use is to inform our hearer that he may rely on our doing something, are often supposed to lay some sort of magical spell on the speaker, which he must never break if he is to keep his morality intact.

Today, however, our love for magic finds expression chiefly in the way in which words are used, not for communication, but as slogans intended to arouse feeling. Politicians and orators in general spend most of their time using words in this way, for it is their business, not to convey logical meaning, but to inspire action. Advertisers practise the same art with equal success. Thus a great number of our words are charged with emotional or magical content. At the time of writing, the word 'Communist' is the prime example. It is believed in some quarters that 'Communist' is a magic word, which acts as a weapon for use against those whom you think to be evil or undesirable. 'Democratic', on the other hand, acts like a slap on the back or a hand-shake: it applies to those who are politically desirable. In Russia, the magic words are different: 'Fascist', 'bourgeois', and 'capitalist' are weapons, 'socialist', 'proletariat' and 'Marxist' are handshakes. In the advertising world, a great effort is made to impress the importance of the names of various products on the public: to give them a magical power. Sometimes this is done by unconscious subtlety, through transferring the emotional content of one phrase to the name of the product. Thus 'Cadbury's means good chocolate' attempts to transfer our approval of good chocolate to Cadbury's chocolate. 'Beer is best' is another example.

Perhaps the most important way in which we are tempted by the magical properties which we assign to words is our love for using abstract nouns and pretending that they 'stand for things'. We have already noticed in the last section that this view cannot be upheld even in the case of the simplest nouns like 'elephant'. Nouns used as slogans, like 'Communism', 'democracy' and so on, are more misleading: but the worst offenders are nouns like 'will', 'conscience' and 'soul'. These words certainly have magical force: their meaning, if any, is very doubtful, and yet we use them freely and cheerfully in our arguments, as if it were well known.

These words are highly dangerous, not because they are abstract but because they have (or are supposed to have) magical content. 'Force', 'gravity', 'mass' and other scientific terms are also abstract; but the way in which their meanings are related to those of concrete terms is given by the scientific theories in which they are used; and it is chiefly for this reason that we rarely feel tempted to invest them with magical powers. But wars have been fought over such words as 'conscience', 'soul', and other religious terms, yet it is not at all clear what the use of such terms may be. Undoubtedly they have a use of some sort: but that use is certainly not to 'stand for' some entity or thing for which they are labels. It is unfortunate that this is still unrecognised by those who dispute with these words; for it means that their disputes are likely to be unsuccessful in point of logic and understanding, although they may be emotionally persuasive as disputes involving magic words always are. We must be continually on our guard to make sure that we know what we are saying.

2. Ambiguity

Most of us have been taught to define our words carefully when arguing: but this is of little help unless we are also able to understand what sort of job we want our dis-

words to do. The muddle produced by ambiguity in dis-cussions and argument is only too apparent at the time of writing. The Communist powers use words in quite different senses from the Western powers, which tends to make communication at a diplomatic level difficult unless each side fully appreciates the other's meaning. Thus 'aggression' for the Communists does not seem to include propaganda, sending military equipment or intelligence into any country, or even providing foreign armies with a body of instructing officers: but in Western eyes all these acts might be properly called 'aggression'.

There was once a man who had arrived at the conclusion that it was right for him to make love to other women besides his wife. His argument was involved, but amounted to the following chain of reasoning:

Most people are unfaithful to their wives in this way, so it is natural.

What is natural is right.

Therefore it is right for me to be unfaithful.

Pressed to define 'natural', he substituted the word 'normal', and claimed that his argument still stood. What he failed to understand was that both words had both a descriptive and evaluative meaning (see last section). They can both be used to mean (i) what most people do, *and* (ii) what it is right to do. He managed to slide from one meaning to the other in his argument, and thus arrived at a false conclusion. This was due to his inability to distinguish the uses of such mixed words as 'natural' and 'normal'. Definition could not help him: only the sort of analysis of usage which we have carried out would have been any good.

This is an instance of the most common and most dangerous form of ambiguity. It is worth quoting another:

Suppose *A* and *B* are arguing about capital punishment. *A* says that it is right for a man who has killed another man to be killed himself; *B* denies it. *A* could argue as follows:

(i) It is just for a man to suffer what he made others suffer, i.e. to be punished according to his crime.

(ii) What is just is right.

(iii) Therefore a man who has made another suffer death should suffer death himself.

This argument is fallacious, for the same reason as the argument using the word 'natural'. For 'just' means *both* 'according to the principle of retribution' (its <u>descriptive</u> meaning) *and* 'right' (<u>evaluative</u>). In statement (i) of his argument, *A* uses only the descriptive meaning, and in (ii) and (iii) he proceeds to make use of its evaluative meaning also, in a misleading way. *B* should object at statement (ii). He could say 'I admit that the principle of retribution is "just", but only in the descriptive sense of that word: I do not admit that it is "just" in the sense of "right"'.

We can only avoid fallacious argument of this kind by analysing the words used, and by detecting those words which are a <u>mixture</u> of <u>descriptive</u> and <u>evaluative</u> meaning. This is particularly important, because it is usually just those words which we like to argue with; for they represent ideals which many people support, and which may be called into question. Unless we make this analysis, and perceive the mixture, we shall find it impossible to argue effectively about many topics. For many arguments are arguments about what is good and bad, and hence we are likely to employ a great many mixed words of this kind.

In this, as in all other matters, we have to remember to find out the *use* of the word, rather than to investigate its meaning without consideration for the context in which it is used. We have already noted (section A) that words do not have single, standardised meanings apart from their uses, even though it is true that we have agreed to use certain signs in certain ways. It follows, therefore, that within this overall pattern of agreement the actual uses of any word may vary considerably from person to person, and from society to society. This is particularly true of evaluative words, and especially of mixed words such as we have just been considering. The words 'tyrant' and 'pirate' for example, are both words which we now use to show our disapproval of someone's actions. To us, a 'tyrant' is a ruler who rules in an evil way, and a 'pirate' is someone who makes his living in an evil way. But to the ancient Greeks, neither of the corresponding Greek words carried any element of disapproval or condemnation at all. They were simply descriptive.

These changes in use usually occur in a word's evaluative meaning, because different people and societies commend and disapprove of different things, whereas the things which they wish to describe remain fairly constant. Thus both the Russians and the Western world understand the descriptive meaning of the word 'totalitarian', and when they use the word they are both describing the same thing. But to us 'totalitarian' is a mixed word, carrying with it an element of disapproval, whereas to the Russians it has no such implications.

These mixed words, and the constant variation in their use, make it very difficult for us to be unambiguous. For their function is not to clarify any particular question, but rather to pronounce judgment upon it. If we are arguing about whether something is good or bad, right or wrong, it obviously will not do for us to use too many mixed words, for the use of these words begs the question at issue. Supposing, for instance, that we were discussing the case of a beggar who took food from a shop without paying for it in order to save himself from starvation. A most natural comment on this case would be 'That's stealing'. But this only confuses the issue, because the word 'stealing' does not leave it open to anyone else to approve of the beggar's action: for we all use the word to condemn or disapprove of an action. If we really want to approach the question with open minds, we shall avoid such words and keep our *descriptions* of what the beggar has done quite separate from our *evaluation* of what he has done. Nothing is gained by discussing whether it is 'really' stealing or not. We are agreed about what in fact he has done (i.e., we agree that he has 'stolen' in the descriptive sense), but we are not agreed about how this action is to be evaluated (i.e., we are not agreed that he has 'stolen' in the evaluative sense). To try and settle moral questions with words like 'stealing', 'lying' and so on is simply to bow down before the weight of custom and tradition, which prefer to regard the question as already settled. Such customs, and the words they express themselves in, may help to keep society stable, but they are no good for answering genuine questions.

From all these examples, we can see that one of the most dangerous sources of ambiguity arises from the inability to distinguish descriptive from evaluative meaning. The other chief source is the inability to distinguish the widely differing uses of descriptive words, and in particular of nouns. Let us first take an example.

During the Second World War, and the years immediately preceding it, the Germans developed a theory about the superiority of 'Aryan blood', in virtue of which they asserted the supremacy of the 'Aryan' races as against Latin, Semitic, Slavonic and other peoples. They used this theory to justify their attempted domination (and in some cases extermination) of non-Aryans like the Jews. Certain American students, presumably intending to discredit the theory, sent Hitler various specimens of blood, each specimen being taken from a member of a different race, including one from an Aryan. They then challenged him to tell which one came from the Aryan. Neither Hitler nor his scientists were able to do so, because there is in fact no such thing as 'Aryan blood': that is, there is no special quality in the blood of Aryans which distinguishes it from the blood of other races.

An intelligent supporter of Hitler would probably have said: 'When we speak of "Aryan blood", you must not understand us too literally. We do not mean that the actual blood of Aryans is anything special. All that we mean is that Aryans are superior to non-Aryans.' Undoubtedly many Germans appreciated this point: but their leaders continued to use the phrase 'Aryan blood', because it had considerable emotional appeal for their followers. 'Blood' is a word which we tend to invest with magical force. Many people, however, took the Germans' assertions quite literally, as the American students may have done, including many of the Germans themselves. This is not difficult to appreciate, when we remember how seriously we used to take the so-called 'blue blood' of our own aristocracy, and how most people did indeed think that there was something actually in the blood of kings and nobles which was substantially different from the blood of commoners.

These people never seriously asked themselves the question 'What is the precise use of the descriptive word "blood"?' For if they had done so, they would have been forced to say, either that it referred literally to the red stuff in our veins, or that it had a more abstract use. In the first alternative, they would have been impelled to satisfy their curiosity by testing their assertion, as the American students did: in the second, they would have had to face the question of what the actual use of 'blood' was, and they would have had to answer this question before making any assertions about it. In other words, it was only by preserving the ambiguity of the word that they were able to make and believe in these curious assertions.

Consider now another common descriptive word, the word 'intelligence'. People will often argue about whether or not animals have intelligence. *A* will say: 'Oh yes, my dog is very intelligent: he barks to go out for a walk, and brings me the newspaper in the morning.' *B* replies: 'No, animals can't have intelligence; they can't talk, and they don't understand when you ask them questions.' And so the argument often continues. The word 'pain' produces similar arguments. *A* says: 'Animals certainly feel pain, look how they squeal and writhe when they're hurt: they feel pain just as you or I do.' *B* answers: 'Of course they can't feel pain: why, they're not conscious at all.' All these arguments revolve primarily about what it is that the descriptive words are supposed to describe. *A* thinks that 'intelligence' describes certain types of action, like barking to go out for a walk, bringing home newspapers and so on; and that 'pain' describes whatever feeling lies behind squealing and writhing. *B*, on the other hand, thinks that the words have to describe more than these. To him, intelligence must describe the ability to talk and understand; pain must describe something felt by a conscious mind. *A* and *B* are really arguing about the proper use of the words: for they may be in perfect agreement about the observed facts. They may be of one mind about what is to be described (barking to go out, squealing and writhing, etc.):

but they evidently differ about what descriptive word to use. Until they realise the purely verbal nature of their argument, it is likely to be inconclusive.

Most of these ambiguities occur in the case of abstract words, because as we have seen people like to think that they are arguing about the 'things' which the words 'stand for'. When they discuss justice, or intelligence, or conscience, they regard their discussion in the light of a treasure hunt, in which everyone involved is expected to hunt around until they find justice, or intelligence, or conscience: and when they have found it, they can then identify it for their friends. To take another analogy, they think that there are 'things' labelled 'justice', 'intelligence' and so on, and that all they have to do is to get other people to see the thing and read the labels: and if the others cannot do this, they must be either blind or obstinate. In actual fact, of course, they should not be arguing about this at all. The truth is that they are not agreed about their use of descriptive words. No doubt it is profitable to discuss the matter, in order to reach agreement about their use; but this is a very different sort of discussion. Once we see that it does not matter what words we use to describe what, provided that we agree about the uses, these arguments seem rather foolish.

In some cases the ambiguity in the use of descriptive words is so gigantic that it is not noticed at all, simply because we do not bother to find out what is being described. If I gave as a reason for why the room was cold, the explanation that it was due to the low temperature, it would be objected that I had not explained anything at all: for 'cold' and 'low temperature' are simply two ways of describing the same thing. Yet a similar mistake was actually committed by the first doctors who attempted to investigate the properties of opium. Opium puts people to sleep: and they offered as an explanation of this the view that it had a *vis dormitiva* or 'soporific quality'. Of course we can see that this is no explanation: it is just saying that opium puts people to sleep because it puts people to sleep, which is not very helpful. In other words, no new facts are being described by the phrase *vis dormitiva*. Yet the 'explanation' was swallowed, because *vis dormitiva* was thought to describe something new; some special 'thing' inside opium which had been discovered: though perhaps it would be better to say that most people did not really think about what the phrase described at all. If they had, they would have seen that it described either the already-known fact that opium puts people to sleep, or some new fact. In the first case it would not serve as an explanation, and in the second they would want to know something about this fact—at least, whether it *was* a fact.

The ambiguities in the use of descriptive words are so numerous that we can do no more than note a few examples from various fields of discussion. First, in the fields of psychology and education, we can take numerous instances from any book or discussion. We have already noticed 'intelligence'. Other such words are 'instinct', 'heredity', 'discipline', 'sanity', 'complex'. In politics, always a fruitful field for vague descriptive words, we might quote 'state', 'law', 'rights', 'freedom' and many others. In religion, we have 'will', 'soul', 'conscience', 'sin' and 'grace', not to mention what we might call 'supernatural' words like 'God', 'hell', 'heaven' and so forth. Even science is not free from ambiguities attaching to words like 'universe', 'life', 'time' and 'space'. With all these words, our task is to determine their use: and this can only be done by asking ourselves what precisely we are trying to describe or explain by them—what experiences we intend to group together when we use them. For if we do not know what experiences we want to describe or explain, when we use descriptive words, then—to put it bluntly—we cannot really know what we are talking about.

It is worth pointing out that a great many such words, which seem ambiguous to the layman, are often used quite unambiguously by experts within their own particular branch of knowledge. Thus words like 'sin' and 'sacrament' are often used loosely and ambiguously by ordinary people; but the clergy of any one Christian sect might use them clearly and consistently in accordance with official definitions. 'Sacrament', for instance, is defined by the Catechism in the Book of Common Prayer as 'an outward and visible sign of an inward and spiritual grace'. Again, a statement like 'the universe is expanding' seems to suggest that in physics the word 'universe' lacks the ambiguities which it has in common speech. If 'universe' means 'everything that there is', a layman might ask, how can it possibly expand? It would have no room to expand into. Yet it is possible, even for the non-scientist, to see that the statement is not so absurd as it sounds. Imagine a small creature, whose experience was confined to two dimensions only, crawling round a balloon. The surface of that balloon is *his* universe. Increase the surface area of the balloon by blowing it up more, and you have increased the size of his universe: his universe has expanded. Perhaps, then, it would be more accurate to say that *our* universe is expanding. Whether or not this statement is true, nobody can say for certain. But it is plain enough that we can only understand it by learning the particular sense in which 'universe' is used; and we cannot hope to do this without learning something of the science of physics, which has given it this particular sense.

It is extremely difficult to avoid making mistakes about words. Magic and ambiguity are often too strong for us. To define them, or to agree with somebody else about their meaning, is usually inadequate: for to define or agree about meanings is often only to substitute one vague word or phrase for another. We may agree that 'natural' means 'normal', that 'God' means 'the Omnipotent Creator', that 'soul' means 'the inner self', that 'sin' means 'misuse of the will', without reaching any more understanding or clarity whatsoever. Indeed, we often substitute these words in order to avoid having to analyse what we are saying. It is very easy to be vague, emotional, persuasive, sincere, fluent and supposedly 'reasonable'. In this country, perhaps, we distrust emotional appeals, and prefer an honest, sincere and unrhetorical speech from the heart. But that does not mean we are any the less confused. People usually resent their views, and the statements in which they express them, being subjected to any analysis or critical investigation: and naturally, they hate being told that (literally) they do not understand what they are talking about. Yet until they learn to avoid confusion in their words, arguments are bound to be fruitless.

In order to succeed, it is essential to become *conscious* of words. Most of the time we use words unconsciously, without thinking what we are saying. If we can become conscious of them, and interested in them for their own sake and for the sake of the jobs they do, we shall be well on the road to understanding. And if we can do the same with statements, we shall have equipped ourselves with an effective method of discovering truth and knowledge.

CHAPTER II

STATEMENTS

A. THE FUNCTION OF STATEMENTS

LIKE words, statements are tools; or rather they are sets of tools, with each set designed to do a different job. Like words, again, they do these jobs because we use them as signs; or rather as complex groups of signs. Just as we might use a spanner and a car-jack for changing a wheel on a car, so we might use two words together for the purpose of communicating something. In this chapter we shall consider how to recognise and analyse these sets of tools, and how to distinguish one set from another.

Our communications may be grouped under two main headings, which it will be best to consider at once.

1. Poetic communication

We have already noticed certain uses of words when we observed the use of interjections in the last chapter (section B, 4). We saw that some words like 'Blimey!' or 'Good heavens!' were not meant to be taken literally. This is an example of what I shall call 'poetic communication'. By this I mean communication where the literal and prose sense of the words has either secondary importance, or no importance at all. In other words, we are not trying in this form of communication to make logical sense at all: we are simply trying to *express* something. This is a genuine form of communication, but it is quite different from other forms.

47

Nobody really knows how poetic communication works, or why certain communications have a strong emotional appeal to so many people: it is agreed only that it is quite different from logical communication. It demands a different response. When Keats says 'Thou wast not born for death, immortal Bird!' in his Ode to a Nightingale, he does not intend seriously to inform us that nightingales (or even one nightingale) are immortal. The reader who said 'That's silly, nightingales only live a few years' would be rightly regarded as missing the point, because he does not understand the nature of Keats's communication. Again, when Donne writes 'Go and catch a falling star', readers are not expected to carry out his commands. Catching falling stars is impossible, and Donne knows it. His true meaning in the poem is 'Just as it is impossible to catch a falling star, so you cannot find a constant woman anywhere'. That is his *prose* meaning: but this meaning is only secondary. He wishes, not to inform us of feminine psychology, but to arouse our feelings in some way.

We are only concerned with poetic communication because it tends to intrude itself into prose or logical communication. The two are indeed very difficult to distinguish, but the distinction must be made if we are to assess our communications correctly. Not infrequently the same communication has both a poetic and a prose sense, and it is difficult to say which is subordinate. For example, when the writer of the psalms says 'God is our hope and strength, a very present help in trouble. Therefore will we not fear though the earth be moved, and though the waters be carried into the midst of the sea', he is both writing poetry of high quality and making a serious and literal assertion of faith. Milton, speaking of God the Son, writes 'Before, the stars, Before the sun Thou wert, and at the voice Of God as with a mantle did'st invest The rising world of waters dark and deep Won from the void and formless infinite'. This is both poetry and logical communication. The speeches of famous statesmen like Abraham Lincoln and Burke, while perhaps not exactly poetic in quality, evidently *express* a great deal more than they *mean*: our response is emotional as well as logical.

From our point of view we are only concerned to ensure that we can distinguish one sort of communication from the other. The beliefs of men, and perhaps particularly their religious beliefs, tend to seek expression in the most poetic form. The greatness of the Bible, for instance, lies not least in its high literary value. Prayers, political songs and slogans, proverbs and moral injunctions, and formalised ritual sayings of all kinds tend to acquire poetic force. This is desirable for many reasons, provided only that we do not lose sight of their prose meaning. Pure poetry is one thing; nobody 'takes it seriously'. Pure prose, such as a scientific text-book, is another; nobody feels inclined to read it in the sing-song, faintly mystical voice which we reserve for poetry. But mixed communication are dangerous, for we may easily allow their poetic force to blind us to the prose meaning. And if we are supposed to take the prose meaning seriously, we may very well find ourselves not knowing what our own beliefs mean, or whether they are true.

2. *Prose communication*

Prose communication consists of words of which we are intended to make logical sense: words which we are supposed to understand with our reason, not appreciate with our feelings. It is with this sort of communication that we shall be concerned, because this is the type of communication which we ought to use in arguing, discussing, solving problems, and discovering truth. Of course it has many other uses besides these. We use it to state facts, express fears, hopes and wishes, give commands, make decisions, ask questions, and so on. Some of these questions, but not all, are used for discovering truth.

To gain a rough idea of the various types of prose communication, we can list a number of sentences all of which include some reference to the same event. We can then see the different uses which our language enables us to make of this event.

1. You are shutting the door.
2. Are you shutting the door?
3. Shut the door!
4. You ought to shut the door.
5. May you shut the door soon!
6. You didn't shut the door.

These could be paraphrased in the following way, putting the event first and our handling of the event or way of communicating it afterwards:

1. Shutting the door by you: yes, it's going on now.
2. Shutting the door by you: is it going on now?
3. Shutting the door by you: yes, please!
4. Shutting the door by you: yes, I commend it to you.
5. Shutting the door by you: I hope it will happen soon.
6. Shutting the door by you: no, it didn't happen.

The ways in which we handle the event 'shutting the door by you', as they appear in the first list, are woven into the texture of the sentence: yet the logic and sense of the sentences is quite different. It is this logical sense in which we are chiefly interested. In the second list, the last part of each sentence, as we have written them, has a purely logical function. The words in it are nearly all 'pointer words' (see section B of the last chapter).

Statements

Before considering the actual types of statements in prose communication, we have first to make plain an important principle, which is not only the best method of distinguishing one type of statement from another, but also throws light upon each individual type.

B. VERIFICATION

'Verification' means finding out whether something is true. I shall speak also of the 'method of verification', which means simply the way in which you find out whether something is true. The 'something' is usually a statement, although it may be a belief. For example, if I told you that there was a hippopotamus in the next room, you might want to find out whether that was true, to verify it. You would go and look, or send somebody to look for you: either of these would be good methods of verification. Or if I told you that 9 x 9 was 81, and you were not sure that this was true, you could verify it by calculation.

It is important to attend to the method of verifying any statement for two reasons: verification is a guide to meaning, and it is also a guide to truth. I have given these two reasons in order of importance. Supposing we wanted to find out whether a certain statement was true. In order to be sure of getting the right answer, we should have to go through the following process:

(i) Discover the meaning of the statement, i.e. what its use is and what sort of thing it is intended to communicate.

(ii) Agree about *how* to discover whether it is true or not, i.e. about what is to count as acceptable evidence and what is not.

(iii) Consider the evidence and decide.

Most arguments are fallacious or inconclusive, simply because (i) and (ii) are overlooked. People imagine that they already know what their statements mean, and that they are agreed about the methods appropriate to discovering whether they are true or not. In the case of some statements, this may be a reasonable assumption: but as these are not the statements anyone wants to question, this is not very helpful. All statements whose truth is at all doubtful *must* first be dealt with by the process I have outlined: and for going through this process, verification is the only possible guide, as we shall now observe.

(i) Verification is a guide to meaning, because the meaning of a statement depends largely on its method of verification. In the last chapter (section c) we considered a dispute about whether animals were intelligent. The statement under discussion, then, was 'Animals are intelligent'. *A* and *B* could not agree about the truth of this statement. We can now put the nature of their disagreement more precisely: they were not agreed about the proper way to verify the statement. *A* thought that certain things (dogs bringing home newspapers, and barking to be let out) counted as evidence for intelligence: *B* would not accept this. If *A* says 'My dog's intelligent', *B* could have asked 'What do you mean, intelligent?', and *A* could have said 'Well, it brings home the newspaper and barks to be let out'. *B* could then have perceived what *A* meant by 'intelligent', and what *A* thought to be the proper method of verifying the existence of intelligence, for *B* has been given instances of what in *A*'s view counts as intelligence.

Again, the word 'table' means something solid, with legs and a flat top which you can put things on. But these properties also form part of the method of verifying the existence of tables. If you want to know whether there is a table in the next room, then you look for something solid, with legs and a flat top for putting things on. The method of verification is bound up with the meaning: in a way, they are two sides of the same coin. We can find out the use or meaning of a statement by finding out what is supposed to count as verification of it.

Sometimes this brings surprising results. Supposing *A* says 'The soul is immortal'. This is a very vague statement, and we may not reach a satisfactory conclusion about its meaning—about what *A* is trying to communicate—merely by attending to and analysing the individual words. But if we ask what sort of evidence or verification *A* thinks proper to such a statement, we shall have a better idea of what he is using it for. It may turn out that he would accept *no* evidence against the statement: and this might be because he uses 'soul' to mean 'the immortal part of man', so that it necessarily followed that the soul was immortal, by definition. In that case, we should be inclined to treat *A*'s statement in a very different way. All he is really saying is 'the immortal part of man is immortal'. He is not trying to give us information about the soul: he is simply playing with words. But we could not perceive this without noticing that he will accept no evidence against his statement, and the reasons for his refusing to do so.

Sometimes, again, we can use verification to observe that a statement really has no meaning at all. This is the case when neither the speaker nor anyone else can think of any sort of evidence which would count for or against its truth. Supposing, for instance, I say 'My dog is squmpish', but can give no indication of how to tell when a dog is squmpish or not, I am probably talking nonsense. If nothing is to count as being squmpish, then the word 'squmpish' does not have any conceivable use or meaning.

The dog might equally well not be squmpish: nobody would notice any difference. If there is no possible method of verification, then there is no meaning.

(ii) Verification is a guide to truth, for the more obvious reason that we must agree about how to find out whether a statement is true before discussing it. Often we are so agreed. If I said 'There is a hippopotamus in the next room', it would be proper for you to answer 'No, because I went in and looked everywhere and couldn't see one'. But it would be silly to answer 'No, because it's raining'. That would not be a good reason, because it shows ignorance of the proper way of verifying the existence of a hippopotamus. If I had said 'We don't need our mackintoshes today', of course it would be quite proper to say 'No, you're wrong, we do need them because it's raining'. Each statement has its own proper verification.

To take a more important example, men have not always agreed about the method of verifying the statement 'The world is round'. Before Galileo, it was considered appropriate to say 'No, the world is flat, because you can see that it is, and anyway the Bible says so'. But now we prefer to rely upon scientific observation. We have adopted a different method of verification. It would obviously be pointless to argue for any length of time with someone who adopted the old method of verification about whether the earth was flat or round. The only profitable approach would be to discuss first which method of verification to use, and only afterwards to apply the method.

It would be wrong to suppose that the way in which we verify statements is always direct and straightforward, as it is in the cases of 'It is raining' or 'There is a hippopotamus in the next room'. The statements of science, of history, and of all other branches of study which have built up our everyday observations into a complex system of laws and hypotheses, require a type of verification which is much more sophisticated than simply using our eyes. A statement like 'The emperor Augustus was faced with two serious conspiracies during his reign' can only be verified by a careful study and a proper understanding of contemporary documents, coins, inscriptions, and so forth. Similarly statements about the chemical composition of water, the distances of stars, the behaviour of light-waves, etc. depend upon highly-organised methods of verification, involving a deep knowledge of the sciences concerned. It is for this reason that we have experts to carry out this verification for us, on whose findings we generally rely; for it would be difficult for a non-expert to master all the necessary knowledge. At their lowest level, admittedly, these sophisticated methods of verification consist simply of sense-experiences. Science is simply organised commonsense; but the organisation is often very complex.

Nearly all important arguments turn on the method of verification of the statements involved. Their truth depends on whether they can pass certain tests: and it is necessary to agree about what tests the statements must pass. If *A* thinks that a statement need only agree with the Bible, *B* that it need only agree with the scientists, *C* that it need only agree with his 'conscience', and so on, no progress will be made in an argument between them, unless the argument first tackles the question of which tests are the proper ones. We may disagree about this, but at least we shall know where we stand.

We can now investigate the particular types of statements, paying particular attention to their method of verification, which will help us to assess their use and purpose.

C. TYPES OF STATEMENTS

1. Imperatives and attitude—statements

By these I mean statements used to give commands, or express the speaker's wishes, hopes, desires, fears, and so forth; for example, 'Serve God, and honour the king!', 'Down with the aristocrats!', 'I hate Communists', 'Let us love all men as brothers', 'I feel humble in a cathedral'. These statements form a class on their own, because they are either not verifiable at all, or only in a trivial way. This is not because they have no use or meaning, as was the case with 'My dog is squmpish' (see section B). It is rather because they are not the sort of statements intended to be true or false, except in a trivial sense: they are rather expressions of attitude, or commands. Thus 'Serve God!' is not true or false: we just do not want to apply those standards to it. In one sense, it is not a statement at all (although it is a sentence): it is a command. 'I hate Communists' is true or false in the unimportant sense that either I do hate Communists or I do not: but the main use of the statement is to express my attitude. I might just as well have said 'Down with Communists!', without really altering the meaning of the statement.

These statements, or sentences, are important, because they represent the intrusion of what I called poetic communication. They are not intended to state facts, or to give information about the world: they simply express the speaker's feelings or desires. They are, therefore, of no possible value in argument or discussion: because in these activities we are trying to get at the truth, not to express our feelings. But they are of interest to us, chiefly because what appear to be other kinds of statements may really be imperatives or attitude-statements in disguise.

For example, a statement like 'All men are equal', or 'All men are born free' looks like a straightforward indicative statement, whose use is to convey certain information about the world. They look parallel to statements such as 'All men are mortal' or 'All men are born with two eyes in their heads'. But if we examine them more closely, we can see that they are not used in the same way at all. For what sort of information is conveyed by the statement 'All men are equal'? Is one supposed to verify such a statement by measuring the various properties of men—their height, their intelligence, their virtue, and so on—and seeing whether they are equal? In what particular respects are they supposed to be equal? Again, how do you verify the statement 'All men are born free?' What counts as being 'born free' and not being 'born free'?

Such statements are really disguised attitude-statements; though of course other uses may be found for them, these will be secondary uses. 'All men are equal' is used rather as the attitude-statement 'Down with privilege!' is used. In history we find that men make such statements as protests against particular types of privilege which disqualify them from doing certain things: for instance, against class-privilege, the colour bar, the privileges of the wealthy, and so on. Similarly 'All men are born free' is a protest against various types of tyranny or compulsion, and is used to mean 'Away with this tyrannical behaviour!' These statements do not really give information at all: they express attitudes.

We have to pay attention to the context of such statements, before we can decide upon their use. Even then we may not be certain: but at least we can ask the speaker what he intends to convey, and how his statement is supposed to be verified. But in most cases the attitude is sufficiently obvious for us to classify them as attitude-statements. When the French revolutionaries, for instance, insisted on the value of liberty, equality and fraternity, they did so as a protest against certain forms of tyranny practised by the nobles (lack of liberty), the nobles' privileges (lack of equality), and their ill-treatment and discourtesy at the nobles' hands (lack of fraternity). Most statements about liberty, equality and fraternity are disguised attitude-statements, protesting against certain behaviour.

It is often difficult to decide whether certain statements are attitude-statements or not. This is particularly true in the case of religious or 'metaphysical' statements (see part 5 of this section). But we can always discover how a statement is to be treated by discovering how it is to be verified. Thus 'God is a loving father' *might* be an attitude-statement, meaning 'Let us love each other as brothers' or 'Let us feel grateful for the good things of life'. Alternatively, it might be giving information, in which case we should want to know what sort of information, and how to tell what counts as evidence for its truth. The onus of giving an account of the meaning and verification of a statement which purports to give information lies on the person who makes the statement. If he cannot do this, we may feel inclined to say that it does not really give information, and is not the sort of statement to call true or false: that it is just an attitude-statement.

2. *Empirical statements*

An empirical statement is one which gives information about the world, based on our experience of it. ('Empirical' comes from the Greek word for experience.) Many statements are of this kind, such as 'All swans are white',

'London is in England', 'The earth is going round the sun', 'It will rain tomorrow', and so on. We can say, perhaps, that empirical statements state facts about the world of our experience.

They must be distinguished from attitude-statements, and from the other types of statements which we shall consider later. The distinguishing mark of empirical statements is that we verify them by tests conducted in terms of our experience: and ultimately, in terms of our sense-experience. In other words, we make observations in the world and decide whether the statement is true or false. Another distinguishing mark is that no empirical statement *must* be true in point of logic, nor need it necessarily be false for logical reasons. We may be certain of their truth, but it is our experience that has made us certain, not any rule of logic. Thus we may be certain that the statements 'The sun will rise tomorrow' or 'All men are mortal' are true: but there would be nothing *logically* odd about the sun not rising tomorrow, or finding a man who was immortal. It would be curious, but not logically curious. It is not impossible in the strictest sense, though we may call it impossible in the looser sense, meaning that it is so unlikely as to be virtually out of the question. On the other hand, the statement 'All men are human beings' is necessarily true, for we have so defined 'men' in our language that 'men' means 'human beings'. To say 'this man is not a human being' is logically absurd: it is self-contradictory. Similarly, if $a = b$, and $b = c$, then it is logically necessary that $a = c$. This has nothing to do with experience: it is a matter of logical rule.

We can also classify empirical statements in a way which we cannot use for other statements. To verify an empirical statement, we have a series of tests which we can carry out:

thus to verify a statement like 'It will rain tomorrow', we might use a barometer, the Air Ministry weather report, whether Aunt Jemima's big toe is aching, whether seaweed is dry or wet, and so on. If all these tests support the statement 'It will rain tomorrow', we might feel inclined to say that it was 'certain' that it would rain: if most of them supported it, we could say that it was 'probable': and so we could go on, and classify the statement as 'quite likely', 'possible', 'improbable', 'highly unlikely' or 'virtually impossible', according to the evidence we had for its truth. We cannot do this with other statements.

3. *Analytic statements*

Analytic statements do not give information about the world or about our sense-experiences at all. They are statements whose verification is not to be found in experience, but in seeing whether or not they obey certain logical rules. This can be seen directly in the simplest cases, but usually it has to be done by seeing whether or not they can be deduced from the simplest analytic statements.

We have already given instances of analytic statements, such as 'All men are human beings'. In making this statement, we are obviously not intending to tell our hearers something important about men, as we should be if we said 'All men have two eyes in their heads'. Again, if we said 'Everything that is red is coloured', we should not be giving information about the colour red, as if we had said 'Everything that is red is dangerous'. 'Figures with three sides are triangles' does not tell us anything useful about figures with three sides: 'Things never fall upwards' does not give us any new facts about things falling.

What, then, is the use of these statements, since they do not describe our experiences in the world of hard fact?

They are used very much as the propositions of mathematics and geometry are used: namely, to show how we have agreed to relate the meanings of verbal signs to one another. 'All men are human beings' does not tell us anything about men: but it does tell us about the word 'men'. It tells us that the verbal sign 'men' and the sign 'human beings' are logically equivalent: that the one entails the other. Similarly 'Everything that is red is coloured' gives us information about the use of words: it tells us that if we want to use the sign 'red', we must, by the rules of language, also be prepared to use the sign 'coloured' with reference to the same object. 'Red' entails 'coloured'. Similarly, 'Figures with three sides are triangles' simply gives us a word to use ('triangle') in place of another verbal sign ('three-sided figure'). 'Things never fall upwards' is against the rules: 'fall' necessarily entails 'downwards', and so 'fall upwards' is self-contradictory.

We can see the difference between empirical and analytic statements most clearly if we consider the two statements '2 + 2 = 4', and 'put two oranges next to two other oranges, and you will have four oranges'. The first is analytic: it tells us simply that the signs '2 + 2' and '4' are logically equivalent. The second tells us a fact: it is true, but it is not true because of logical rules only. It is a fact of experience: not a fact of logic. '2 + 2 = 4' is true just because we have *made* it true, because we have so defined our arithmetical signs that the statement necessarily follows. Nothing could ever occur to make us doubt that 2 + 2 = 4. On the other hand, there are plenty of cases where two things added to two other things do not result in four things. Two drops of water added to two other drops of water in the same test tube result in only one drop: and if you take two icebergs from the Arctic Sea, and two more from the Antarctic, and put them all in the Sahara, there will soon be no icebergs at all.

The fact that we should never accept any evidence from the outside world as telling against any analytic statement is important, for it shows that these statements are purely symbolic. By this I mean that they depend for their truth on a man-made set of rules, and follow logically from human definitions. Arithmetic and algebra are simply manipulations of sets of symbols which we ourselves have contrived; although these manipulations are very useful. Geometry is even more obviously not dependent on what we experience. According to our axioms, for instance, a line has length but no thickness. In the world of experience no such thing exists, for all lines have some thickness, however carefully we draw them. We never meet with perfect triangles, circles and squares in the world: indeed, we never meet them anywhere. They simply act as symbols: and all the proofs of the theorems in geometry follow logically upon our axioms. We can deduce them merely by the laws of logic and language.

Analytic statements are useful because they allow us to make useful deductions, and enable us to deduce one empirical statement from one or more others. They act as a kind of logical tool which helps us to do our thinking. Although their truth does not depend on experience, they enable us to transform one piece of empirical knowledge into another. This is particularly true of mathematical statements. Thus from the statements 'I have two apples in my right hand' and 'I have two apples in my left hand', we can deduce the statement 'I have four apples altogether': and we can do this, because we know that the analytic statement '$2 + 2 = 4$' is true. Most mathematics, of course, involves more sophisticated deductions than this. But without these deductions, and the analytic statements which represent them, we should have no mathematics, and consequently no science and no economics.

If we are now clear what an analytic statement is, we can see how often such statements occur, often without the speaker's knowledge, in the course of argument or discussion. Sometimes it is not clear whether a statement is analytic or not: and then we have to discover how the speaker verifies it—whether he brings in evidence from the outside world, or simply points to the rules of language and logic. 'The soul is immortal' is analytic if the speaker uses 'soul' in such a way that it logically follows that it is immortal. If 'soul' means 'the immortal part of man', then his sentence can be analysed into 'the immortal part of man is immortal'. This gives us some help about how he is using the word 'soul', but that is all. But if he does not mean by 'soul' something that logically entails being immortal, then his statement is not analytic.

Analytic statements are not, of course, always necessarily true. But in that case they are self-contradictory. If I say '9 × 9 = 83', and intend this to be verified by the rules of arithmetic, then the multiplication tables will show me to be wrong. 'A puppy is a young dog' gives true information about the word 'puppy': but 'A puppy is a young cat' gives false information. Statements like 'A triangle has four sides' are self-contradictory: they break the rules of language and logic.

It is important to recognise analytic statements, or rather statements which are used analytically, because they frequently appear in arguments under disguise; as in the case of 'The soul is immortal'. Consider another example. *A* says 'Everyone's motives for acting are always selfish'. Now this looks like an empirical statement. *B* says: 'What about martyrs who die for their cause, or people who sacrifice their own happiness and desires for the good of others?' *A* replies 'Oh, well, these are really selfish motives: after all, these people *want* to act in this way. They're doing what they desire to do, and that's selfish.' At this point it becomes clear that *A* is using the word 'selfish' in a curious way: in a way from which it logically follows that his original statement was true. In his language, to call a motive 'selfish' does not distinguish it in any way: if a man has a motive, it must logically be 'selfish', because this is what he wants to do. So *A* is really saying 'Everyone's motives for acting are motives'. This tells us that *A* is using 'selfish' in a curious way. He will not accept any evidence against motives being selfish, because (to him) motives are selfish, not in point of fact, but because of the meanings of the words. His statement is therefore analytic.

Analytic statements may also be disguised, not as empirical ones, but as statements of value (see next section). Certain statements, which might seem to be statements of value, are obviously analytic. If I ask 'What ought I to do?' and you answer 'You ought to do what is right', you have not helped me at all, for your answer gives no information to me. You are simply saying 'You ought to do what you ought to do': for it is in accordance with the rules of language that 'right' can be substituted for 'what you ought to do'. But with other words the disguise is more effective. If you had answered 'You ought to do your duty', this may be analytic. It may be that you are using 'duty' to mean simply 'what you ought to do'. Alternatively, you may mean by 'duty' a number of specific things, like always fighting for king and country, obeying your parents, and so on. In that case, your statement may be helpful. It all depends on how you propose to verify 'duty'. If you verify it in the same way as you verify 'what you ought to do', then its meaning is the same, and the statement is analytic. If you verify it by other methods, it may not be.

4. *Value statements*

Value statements must include an evaluative or mixed word (see last chapter, section B, 2); that is, they must use a word whose purpose is to commend or evaluate. They may, indeed, be defined as statements in which evaluative or partly-evaluative words play an important part. 'He is a good man', 'You ought not to do that', 'Democracy is the best form of government' and 'It is right to kill murderers' are all value statements.

In the section on evaluative words I referred to the importance of principles of judgment, or criteria. The criteria of our evaluation of anyone or anything are simply the considerations that influence us when we judge, or the tests which we think a thing has to pass if we are to call it good, or commend it, or assign value to it. Thus for most people today the 'criteria of goodness' for men—the considerations that influence them when they are wondering whether to call someone good or not—include such tests as whether he is kind, whether he is honest, brave, straightforward, good-tempered, and so forth. These criteria are really the method of verifying our value statements.

When we use evaluative words and make value statements, we are commending something or somebody. But this is not just adopting an attitude towards the subject of our commendation. To say 'Joe is a good man' is not like saying 'Good old Joe!'. The former is a value statement, the latter an attitude-statement. The former has a method of verification, the latter has not. Value statements are not attitude-statements. It is undoubtedly true that when we make value statements, we are adopting an attitude of approval: but it is not our only or even our main object to express this attitude when we make the statements. We are also *assigning value*. We do this on the basis of certain criteria: and if challenged, we could give reasons for our belief. We could answer the question 'How do you verify this statement?' by saying 'Well, with me a "good man" is someone who is so-and-so and such-and-such. If he passes these tests, I consider my statement verified.'

As with other statements, so with value statements: the most important thing is to agree about the proper method of verification. This entails agreeing about the appropriate criteria. In many cases we are agreed: we all have the same criteria for good knives, for instances—that they should cut well, stay sharp, not break, and so on. Consequently the statement 'This is a good knife' can be profitably discussed, because we all want the same method of verification used. We simply see whether the knife in question passes the established tests or not. If it does, we agree to call it 'good'. Exactly the same applies to our judgments of men, actions, motives, and societies: though these judgments are *moral* judgments, unlike our judgment about knives. They are both *value-judgments*, however, and they both depend for proof on established methods of verification, or agreement about what criteria to use.

Unfortunately we do not always agree about the criteria or method of verification appropriate to our value statements. Some people may have one set of criteria for what counts as a good man, other people may have a quite different set. Good behaviour is different in Russia and in America, in the Victorian Age and in the twentieth century. If I were arguing over some question of value with a cave-man, for instance, it would become evident that we held entirely different sets of criteria for value. Until we could agree to use the same set, our argument would be ineffective. He would call a man who clubbed women over the head and stole whenever he got the chance a 'good' man: I would call a man who was courteous to women and only stole when he could not get food any other way a 'good' man. There would be an impasse.

We might, of course, proceed a little further with the argument, by arguing not about what men counted as good, but about which of our two sets of criteria was the better. This is a more difficult business: for we should really be discussing which method of verification is more appropriate to our value statements about people. In order to settle the question, we should have to employ higher criteria: or we should have to agree about a method of verification to verify which method of verification was the more appropriate. For instance, I could argue with the cave-man thus: 'If you accept human happiness as valuable, then you must accept not stealing as valuable, because stealing does not bring happiness: and if you accept that, you must accept a man who does not steal as valuable or good, at least in that particular respect'. This argument would only work if he shared my higher criteria for value—namely, whether something brings happiness. If he did not share this, of course, I could not convince him.

We can always go on questioning our criteria or methods of verification: but we shall only get a satisfactory answer if we have some higher criteria or verification in terms of which to answer the question. If we have none, then we shall not know how to answer it at all. In this as in other cases, verification is all-important.

The distinguishing feature of value statements lies in the importance of the criteria for verifying them. If I make an empirical statement, such as 'This man has taken property which is legally another's', such a statement can be conclusively verified by observation and experience. But if I make a value statement, such as 'This man has acted wrongly', we need to do more than just observe what in fact he has done: in order to verify it. By observation, we may be able to *describe* what he has done perfectly: and two people might agree that the description was accurate. But it would still be possible for those two people to disagree about the *value* of the action. They would so disagree, if they did not share a common set of criteria for the value of actions of this sort. Unless they do share these criteria, no amount of facts or accurate descriptions can prove that the action is good or bad.

This difference between empirical and value statements can be made clear if we consider the two statements 'Poppies are red' and 'Abraham Lincoln was a good man'. Supposing somebody chose to deny the first statement, and asserted that poppies were green. We could refute him by pointing out that the vast majority of people had agreed to call them red, that scientists could measure the distribution of wave-lengths in the light they reflect, and show them to be similar to that in the light given off by other red objects, and so on. We would probably end up by saying that he was colour-blind. In other words, we have a standard and agreed method of verifying whether something is red or not: and if somebody ignores or goes against this method, he is simply making a mistake. But if somebody denied the statement 'Abraham Lincoln was a good man', we could not necessarily convince him by the same method. We could, certainly, tell him what Abraham Lincoln did, and describe his life in detail: and this might convince him, if he had not known it before. But equally it might not. He might accept all the facts, and still disagree about the values. His view might be curious, but it would not be logically curious, as it would be logically curious if he accepted all the facts about poppies but still thought they were green.

This is because the meaning of descriptive words, and the truth of empirical statements, is tied down to the established method of verification. We are all agreed about what it is to count as red, flat, square and so on: and if somebody goes against this agreement, he is talking nonsense, because our language has been tailored to fit this agreement. 'Red' means something which most people think red, and which gives off light of a certain wavelength: if somebody calls poppies green, he is not just expressing a difference of opinion, but misusing words. But a man who called Abraham Lincoln 'bad' would not be misusing words: for evaluative words like 'good' and 'bad' are not tailored to fit any one system of verification at all. They are simply used by people in accordance with their criteria: and different people have different criteria. We could put this by saying that people agree about the reasons for describing things, but that they have different reasons for commending or valuing things.

Provided we hold the same set of criteria as another person, however, the facts of the matter are very important. For the argument then turns simply upon whether the subject of the value statement does or does not satisfy the criteria. Thus if A and B were agreed that a man who told the truth and did not deceive people was to be called 'good', *A* could point out that Abraham Lincoln, as a matter of fact, did satisfy these criteria: and *B* would then have to admit that he was good. The verification of value statements thus depends partly upon experience or knowledge of the facts, and partly upon criteria of value. We shall see later how the second of these factors gives rise to serious problems.

5. *Metaphysical statements*

These are statements about whose meaning and method of verification we are not agreed, or which (so far as we can see) seem to have no meaning or method of verification at all. This does not imply, of course, that we can classify them at once as 'meaningless', 'nonsense', or 'unverifiable', and forget about them. For it is always possible both that we may be able to agree about their meaning and method of verification, and that we may be able to give meaning and verification to those statements which at present seem to have none. To call a statement 'metaphysical' is like putting a letter in the 'pending' tray: it means that we do not yet know what it means or how to verify it, and that therefore we must reserve judgment about whether it is true or not.

To illustrate the difference between metaphysical statements and other statements, let us compare the statements 'There are men on Mars' and 'God will save the righteous'. Now people may entirely disagree about whether either of these is true or not: they may even feel very strongly about their truth or falsehood. But in the case of 'There are men on Mars', they are at least agreed about what would count as good evidence for its truth: they have an agreed verification-method. This is not true of 'God will save the righteous'. It is not at all agreed what is to count as good evidence for this statement: indeed, the individual words 'God', 'save' and 'righteous' are very vague, and their use is not established. Because of this lack of agreement about verification, the meaning of the statement is also dubious. For these reasons, we can safely classify it as 'metaphysical'.

'Metaphysic' means literally 'post-physical': and the statements of metaphysics are supposed to inform us about a world which is not the ordinary physical world, but some supernatural region which exists above the world of nature. That is why most metaphysical statements are found in religious writing and doctrine, because religion has the greatest interest in such a world. But there are plenty of non-religious metaphysical statements: statements about 'ideals' such as justice, beauty, truth and so on, statements about 'natural rights', the 'will,' the 'self' and many other things. Whatever the alleged subject-matter of such statements, they are to be classed as 'metaphysical' if their meaning and verification is obscure and not properly established.

Some of these statements may be safely removed from the 'pending' tray, and put into one of the groups which we have already noticed. For although metaphysical statements *look* like empirical statements, or statements of fact (even if the fact is supernatural rather than natural), this may only be a diguise. Many of them can be reduced to attitude-statements (see part 1). 'God is bountiful' may mean only 'Let us be thankful for the good things of life': 'All men have a natural right to practise their own religion' may mean only 'Let us be tolerant to different religions'. Alternatively they may be classified as value statements: the two above may mean 'We ought to be thankful for the good things of life' and 'It is good for all men to be allowed to practise their own religion'. Again, they may be disguised analytic statements. 'God is loving' is analytic if by 'God' we mean 'our loving father', for of course 'Our loving father is loving' is analytically true, i.e. in accordance with the rules of language.

We can only find out what class to put any metaphysical statement in by asking the speaker what the statement means and how to verify it. For example, supposing someone says to us 'God is loving'. If we ask what it means, he may say: 'It means that we ought to love each other as brothers'. If this is the only account he can give, then the statement is a value statement. If on the other hand he makes it plain that the statement is true by definition, then it is analytic. But if he can give us an account of the statement whereby it can be verified by experience, and its truth tested by the tests of experience and observation, then we may be able to accept his statement as empirical.

Only empirical statements can give us genuine information about facts, so that only those metaphysical statements which we find can be classed as empirical can be thought of as informative, in the sense that they tell us important truths which had escaped our notice. Consequently, unless a metaphysical statement can be provided with agreed meaning and agreed verification, it is of no use in communicating truths about any world, natural or supernatural. If the statement turns out to be a value statement, it may of course present us with a certain set of criteria, and ask us to assent to it; or if it is analytic, it may point out to us the way in which metaphysical words are used. But it cannot give us empirically verifiable truth.

Very often it will be found that nobody is in a position to provide metaphysical statements with an agreed meaning and method of verification, and for that reason most metaphysical statements must remain in the 'pending' tray until they yield to further investigation. Even so simple a statement (as it seems) as 'God exists' must be classified as metaphysical, for nobody has yet produced a satisfactory and unambiguous meaning, and an acceptable method of verification, for dealing with the statement: although plenty of people have produced fallacious arguments for proving it true – fallacious, because such arguments do not attend first to meaning and verification, and are hence entirely ambiguous. The statement is not nonsense, but we have so far been unable to agree about giving it any definite sense, or about accepting an established method of verifying whether it is true or not.

We have now gone through all the different types of statements, and this is more than half the battle. For in order to discover what is true and what is not, it is essential to know the meaning and use of any statement which purports to contribute to truth, and how such statements are supposed to be verified. We can then test them against the available evidence, and see whether they hold water.

However, if the various points which we have made about different types of statements and their verification are clear, it should also be clear that a number of important problems remain to be settled. There seems to be no difficulty about attitude-statements, empirical statements, and analytic statements: provided we can recognise them, we can handle them quite easily. This is chiefly because there is no difficulty about the logical status of such statements, and because we are agreed on their verification. We have means of assessing their truth. But there are problems about value statements and metaphysical statements. We might still want to know, for instance, how we come to have our criteria for value statements, and whether there is any possibility of changing them: or whether there is any special method for finding meaning and verification for metaphysical statements—perhaps particularly for the statements found in religious deliefs. So far these points are obscure.

This obscurity is not really to be deprecated, The worst possible thing is to imagine that we know when we do not know: it is far better to confess ignorance than to pretend to false knowledge. And there is little doubt that on some important points, at any rate, we are still groping in the dark. But if we all admit this, there is some chance that together we may find a road to the light.

CHAPTER III

TRUTH

WE shall now try to answer some of the questions raised at the end of the last chapter, and see how our different statements stand in relation to truth. Let us first, however, as befits cautious students of language, investigate the notion of truth itself.

A. THE CONDITIONS OF TRUTH

Truth is always supposed to be something very important and useful: and it is plain enough how advantageous it is for us to know when things are true. We express much the same point when we talk of the importance of 'knowledge', and of men's desire for 'certainty'. Some people want truth and knowledge for its own sake: others, rightly believing that knowledge is power, want it for the advantages it brings. Yet it is doubtful whether many people are properly aware of the uses of the words 'truth', 'knowledge' and 'certainty', together with many other words which express the same meaning.

If these things are as important as we think then it is a matter of prior importance to know what they are, and how to get them. We know enough by now to dismiss the superficial view that they are 'things' which we can find by a sort of mental or spiritual search, rather as we might find a lost ball or a lost umbrella. We shall rather try to answer the question: What does it mean to say that something is 'true', or that one 'knows' or 'is certain of' something? What counts as being 'true', or 'knowing', or 'being certain of'?

Let us confine our attentions for the present to 'true'. In almost all uses of the word, it is applied to statements or beliefs. We say 'That's true', referring to a statement just made by someone else: or else we say 'It's true that . . .'. Sometimes, as when we say 'Christianity is true' or 'The theory of relativity is true', we are referring to a number of beliefs for which we use the shorthand words 'Christianity' and the phrase 'the theory of relativity'. Beliefs, if they are to be expressed at all, must be expressed in statements; and so we can safely say that truth is something which has to do with statements. The supreme importance of the study of language is at once obvious: for if 'being true' is a property of statements, we shall plainly need to know a great deal about the different types of statements, and about how we can tell when they have this property. We have already covered some of this ground in the last chapter.

If I am to be able to say correctly that a statement is true, I must necessarily be able to do three things first:

(i) Know what the statement means.

(ii) Know the right way to verify it.

(iii) Have good evidence for believing it.

Unless these three conditions are satisfied, it would be ridiculous to say that the statement is true. If I say 'It is true that the earth is round' but add either 'I don't know what that statement means', or ' I don't know how one could verify that statement', or 'I have no good evidence for that statement', any of these additions makes my original statement absurd. To say that something is true, therefore, implies all these three conditions.

The same analysis can be applied to the phrases 'I know that . . .' and 'I am certain that . . .', with the minor exception that it may just be possible that the third condition does not apply to 'I am certain that . . .'. I *can* say without too much absurdity 'I am certain that the earth is round, but I have no good evidence for thinking so', rather as one might say 'I am certain that Hyperion will win the Derby, but I have no good evidence for it'. But even this is rather curious. Apart from this exception, the conditions for truth are the same as those for knowledge and certainty: I shall not waste time by repeating the analysis.

I have stated the three conditions in order of logical importance. Obviously we must find the meaning and method of verification for a statement before we can collect evidence for its truth; otherwise, we should not know what we were collecting evidence *for*, or the way to set about collecting it. As students of language, we shall be almost wholly concerned with these first two conditions: that is why in the last chapter we spent so much time classifying statements and observing their verification-methods. For the actual collection of evidence is a different matter altogether: a matter of ordinary or scientific observation. Thus if we take the statement 'The earth is round', it is our business to see that everyone knows the meaning of it, and the right way to verify it: but it is the scientists' business actually to make the observations and find the concrete evidence.

None of these three conditions is more important than another, for they are all essential. But we can note as a matter of historical fact that when the first two are satisfied, satisfying the third is largely a matter of hard work and patient research. This can be exemplified by comparing our progress in discovering truth in various fields. It is commonly and rightly said that man's scientific knowledge has far outstripped his knowledge in the fields of morals, politics, and religion. This is because we are agreed about the meaning and verification of the sort of statements scientists make, and have been so agreed for a long time; for their meaning has been made clear by their use in scientific hypotheses. No logical problems arise in connection with most of them, though some are vague enough to warrant analysis. Consequently, we have been able to get down to the job of making actual observations which we know to be relevant to proving their truth. Because we know the right *method* of verification, we can collect evidence: for we know the sort of evidence we want.

As we may already have seen from the the last chapter, this is not the case with morals, politics or religion. Statements concerned with these topics are usually value statements or metaphysical statements, whose verification is doubtful, together with a number of other types of statements thrown in to add to the confusion. Few people are clear about the meaning and method of verification of such statements: and not many people can even distinguish one type from another. Little wonder, then, that we have not reached much agreement about what is true in these matters: for we have not reached agreement on the first two conditions—what the statements mean, and what is to count as evidence for them. This, perhaps, is why so many people place more faith in science and scientists than they do in moralists, philosophers, politicians or men of religion. The scientists produce results. The others do not.

Let us now run through the list of different types of statements once more, and see how we stand:

(1) Imperatives and attitude-statements.
(2) Empirical statements.
(3) Analytic statements.

(4) Value statements.

(5) Metaphysical statements.

We can notice at once that the first three of these present no problems as regards truth. (1) Imperatives and attitude-statements are not used to convey truth at all: they are simply not the kind of statements which we would ever wish to call 'true' or 'false'. (2) Empirical statements already satisfy the first two conditions for truth, since we know quite well what they mean, and how to verify them: namely, by means of our sense-experience. We are also agreed about what kinds of sense-experience are relevant to determining the truth of various empirical statements (see previous chapter, section B). Thus, certain experiences are relevant for determining or verifying whether it is raining, certain other experiences for verifying whether the earth is round, and so on. We need only to collect the evidence—itself to have the experiences—in order to prove them true or false. (3) Analytic statements also satisfy the first two conditions for truth, since we know what they mean and how they are used, and we also know their method of verification: namely, by deducing them if they are true, or showing them to be self-contradictory if they are false, in accordance with the rules of logic or language. We also know what sort of rules will be used in such deduction, though we may not know how the deduction can be made. Thus, for an analytic statement like '$32 + 99 = 131$', we know that we must use the rules governing the addition of integers; for 'A puppy is a young dog', the definitions of the words given in a reputable dictionary; for 'The sum of the three angles of a triangle is 180 degrees', to the axioms and definitions of Euclid, and the rules of logic by means of which the statement necessarily follows from those axioms and definitions.

But there are important problems connected with value statements and metaphysical statements; and in this chapter we shall try to make some progress towards clarifying their status in reference to the conditions of truth. It is worth observing how this difference between the first three types of statements in our list and the last two affects our discovery of truth and the progress of knowledge. We usually classify our knowledge under various headings, such as 'history', 'chemistry', 'psychology', 'mathematics' and 'languages'. The reason why these departments of knowledge flourish and produce useful results is partly because they use empirical and analytic statements, and hence the conditions of truth can be satisfied. 'History', 'languages' and the various branches of 'science' all spend their time stating or explaining empirical facts: facts about the past doings of people, facts about various languages, facts about the natural world. Pure mathematics is developed by means of a complex system of analytic statements, which enable us to make useful deductions from one set of facts to another.

But as we have already noticed, certain 'branches of knowledge' (or what is supposed to be knowledge) do not seem to flourish in the same way. There are some, of course, like psychology, which are still in their infancy: but this is because they have not yet quite succeeded in establishing their own status. Thus, we do in fact find in the writings of those who call themselves psychologists all kinds of statements: statements of fact, analytic statements, statements of value, and even metaphysical statements and imperatives. But it would be agreed by most reputable psychologists that the job of psychology is to produce laws which explain matters of fact. In other words, psychology is (or should be) a science, which will help us to know more about the minds of men and how they behave, and which should be able to make successful predictions like any other science. I think we all know, at least, what to expect of psychology. If it cannot yet flourish as it ought, it is not because of any logical difficulties of meaning or verification: more probably it is because psychologists have not yet collected enough evidence to be able to give us much information.

The 'branches of knowledge' which should worry us much more are those which deal in value and metaphysical statements. It is precisely in these fields that no progress seems to have been made. Great sages and philosophers, saints and mystics, heroes and moralists have appeared from time to time and tried to tell us the truth about what we ought to do, what God is like, what lies beyond the boundaries of the visible world, and so forth; but though each has many enthusiastic followers, mankind as a whole seems to be no nearer the truth. There has been no united advance on this front. Here, unlike other 'branches of knowledge', no statements are put forward which everyone thinks to be obviously true. The words generally used for those 'branches of knowledge' in which we notice this disturbing lack of progress are 'ethics' and 'metaphysics'. 'Ethics' is the word commonly used to refer to our ideas and discussions about value, and about moral value in particular. Questions about what actions are right, what sort of people and societies are good, and what we ought to do in our dealings with our fellow-men are all 'ethical' questions. 'Metaphysics' is usually employed to refer to our study of truths which are supposed to be supernatural, or in some way divorced from the immediately observable world of nature. Both words refer to 'branches of knowledge' or fields of study. For our purposes, however, we shall be concerned not with a mysterious 'branch of knowledge' called ethics, but with value statements: nor with another 'branch' called metaphysics, but with metaphysical statements. These two types of statements have already been sufficiently defined in the last chapter.

Everybody holds ethical and metaphysical views, and makes value and metaphysical statements. Nearly all our ideas on moral, political or religious questions are expressed in such statements: and these are the very ideas about which we feel the most strongly, and ought to want to learn the most. Unfortunately these are precisely the statements where the most difficulty about meaning and verification arises, as we have already noticed. Questions like 'Is there a God?', 'Ought we to obey the Ten Commandments?', 'Are the doctrines of Communism true?' and 'Is it right ever to fight wars?' are all questions in whose answers we are vitally interested. As we often put it: we want very much to 'get at the truth' of such matters.

I have said before (and shall say again and again, because most people do not seem to have grasped this essential point at all) that our difficulties with these statements arise because they do not satisfy the first two conditions of truth. Since this is so, our next task will be to investigate the nature of these two conditions more thoroughly—to look closely into the nature of meaning and verification, which have served us so well in the case of other statements.

B. THE BASIS OF MEANING AND VERIFICATION

In section A of the first chapter it was pointed out that our use of signs in general, and language in particular, was based on the conventional agreement about how they should be used. We considered the example of a red stop-light, and saw how agreement about the use of a red light led to our ability to use it with a specific meaning, 'Stop!' We can now see that precisely the same applies to our established methods of verification: this is what we should expect, since verification and meaning are closely bound up with each other. We are agreed about how to verify empirical and analytic statements: the rapid advance of science and mathematics bears witness to this agreement. For the former uses empirical statements, and the latter analytic: and since there are no logical difficulties about verifying or understanding these statements, there are no barriers to progress. Our agreement about empirical statements is particularly well-marked: if it did not exist, we could not ever make true every-day remarks to each other like 'It's raining' or 'The fishmonger has fresh fish today'. Our successful communication depends on our common understanding of the meaning and verification of such remarks.

We must now observe that this agreement is of a special kind. It would be quite misleading to suggest that everyone who can communicate successfully had at some time met together, and decided what the meanings and verification-methods of words and statements were to be. In saying that there is an agreement, we do not mean that men have met together and consciously agreed to use words in a certain way. That would be untrue in point of fact. We mean only that everyone does in fact use words in accordance with a uniform and established set of rules. Of course, we do not often learn these rules consciously, in the case of our own language. We pick up our mother-tongue by imitation and practice. We have not had to face problems of meaning and verification by ourselves. The 'agreement' has grown up by trial and error, in a haphazard way which nevertheless works efficiently in respect of those statements where the agreement holds good.

There are a number of cases, however, where the agreement is genuine, in the sense that it has been consciously arrived at, not merely acquired unconsciously. This usually occurs in the sciences, where it has been found necessary to delimit certain concepts strictly, and to define the words which express them without ambiguity. In chemistry, for instance, there is a clear and unambiguous distinction between what is meant by a 'mixture' and what is meant by a 'compound'; in physics and mechanics the distinction between 'weight' and 'mass', and the meanings of words like 'force', 'work', 'wave' and 'frequency' are all clearly fixed. The student of these sciences has to learn to use their terminology accurately; and the clarity which results is partly the cause of the great advances which have been made by such sciences. Our agreement about this terminology has only been reached after a long process of trial and error; but we know that we ourselves could not grasp the meaning of scientific words by mere practice and imitation, as we pick up the meaning of non-technical words when we are children, simply by listening to our elders talk. We have to do it deliberately and consciously.

It follows, then, that if we are to reach agreement about meaning and verification for value and metaphysical statements, we shall have to reach it consciously: for after thousands of years of human history, during which practically everyone has made such statements, there is no indication that we are coming to such an agreement by practice, or trial and error. This offers the only hope of achieving truth in metaphysics and ethics, for without the agreement there can be no truth. There is no apparent reason why we should not succeed. Changes in our agreement about meaning and verification occur, and can continue to occur: we saw from the statement 'The earth is round', and the way in which its verification altered after Galileo's time, that such changes are possible. Another example is the phrase 'unconscious desires'. This would have been thought nonsense before the time of Freud: but the new data provided by modern psychologists from Freud onwards have enabled us to agree to give it a definite meaning.

These two examples give us the clue to discovering the basis for our agreement about meaning and verification. This basis is twofold. On the one hand, we agree because we have similar experiences. It seems that everyone except those who are colour-blind wishes to make distinctions between their experiences on seeing a poppy, a summer sky, snow, and ripe corn. Because of this similarity of experience, we can agree to use verbal signs for these occasions and many others which seem to be similar also; and in fact we have chosen the signs 'red', 'blue', 'white' and 'yellow'. Galileo's verification was accepted because it was possible for everyone to have the experiences which he had on looking through his telescope at the planets, and to make deductions from them. The meaning of 'unconscious desires' was agreed because the psychologists convinced us that certain observable facts of human behaviour required a new explanation: and the phrase was used to form part of that explanation. On the other hand, we agree because we find such agreement useful or advantageous. We distinguish our experiences primarily for reasons of utility. We find it useful to distinguish sugar from salt, pennies from counters, and chairs from gorse-bushes. We have constructed our conventions of meaning and verification in order to give each other useful information. Galileo's verification was accepted for the same reason that any scientific theory is accepted: because it enables us to predict more accurately, and is more useful to us than the verification used previously. The phrase 'unconscious desires' is accepted because it is useful in explaining psychological illness and in curing it.

Advanced scientific concepts, indeed, are all accepted as meaningful and verifiable primarily because they are useful; and they are useful primarily because they enable us to predict. Prediction is one of the hall-marks of a science, and its usefulness is obvious enough. We depend continually on the reliability of scientific prediction. We are told that if we mix lemon juice with milk the milk will curdle, that if we connect one wire with another our electric lighting will be repaired, that if we use a block and tackle we shall be able to lift a weight much more easily, and so forth. Scientists can predict these things for us from their knowledge of the laws which govern the behaviour of natural phenomena. Most people do not know these laws, and may have little idea of how to verify them for themselves; but they accept that they are verifiable, because they work. It is true, of course, that scientific hypotheses are ultimately verifiable by sense-experience. If we took the trouble, we could have the same sense-experience as expert scientists have: for instance, we could look through telescopes, conduct chemical experiments and so on. But we trust scientific experts, not only because we know that we could have similar experiences to theirs if we wished, but also because their statements usually turn out to be reliable. They produce results. In science also, therefore, our agreement about meaning and verification arises partly from the similarity (or potential similarity) of our experiences, and partly from the obvious usefulness of such agreement.

This view is confirmed from many sources, not least from our observation of young children who are just beginning to talk. They learn first the words that are most useful to them—words like 'Mama' and 'Dadda': and it is evident that their experiences are similar to those of other children, for they are well able to understand each other's use of the signs. Sometimes, indeed, children will actually invent words to refer to their experiences. One boy of sixteen months' age invented the word 'go-go', which he used accurately and consistently to mean any object which he could carry, which had a handle, and which had a lid that would open and shut. He invented this word, because this was the type of object in which he was most interested at the time. Consequently the most *useful* word for him was 'go-go'. He knew what it meant, and how to verify what was a 'go-go' and what was not. Two other children shared a common language consisting of at least two words: 'ee-ee' which meant 'look, something unusual is happening' and 'aw-aw', which meant 'come on, let's swap toys'. Their experiences of unusual things happening, and swapping toys, were the same for both. Hence they agreed to use a common language, and a common standard of verification.

Our problem in dealing with value and metaphysical statements, then, is to see whether we do actually share experiences of a kind which would make it useful for us to agree upon an established meaning and verification for at least some of such statements. Here it is evident that we must begin to distinguish different *types* of experience. Empirical statements are verified, in the last analysis, by sense-experience. Analytic statements are verified by our experience and knowledge of the rules of logic. Can we find different types of experience which can be usefully employed to help us build up a framework of communication for value and metaphysical statements? Let us take them in turn.

C. VALUE STATEMENTS

In the last chapter (section c, 4) we discussed the verification of value statements, and observed that it depended ultimately on our criteria of value, which led us to commend things that had certain descriptive qualities. Thus when we commend a knife as 'good', we have at the back of our minds a set of criteria for judging what is to count as a 'good' or commendable knife—one that cuts well, does not break easily, and so on. We also observed that different people had different sets of criteria for making value statements; and that in some cases we could range sets of criteria in ascending order of importance, using a higher set to justify a lower set, and so on until we arrived at our ultimate criteria of value.

Let us be quite clear about the logical status of these ultimate criteria. Suppose A's ultimate principles for judging whether a state of affairs is good or bad consist of seeing whether there is happiness, life and love: and suppose that B's criteria are precisely the opposite, and consist of the existence of misery, death and hate. Neither A nor B supports any values or moral standards higher than these. In such a case, it looks as if neither can convince the other. For the question between them is 'Is this set of criteria better than that one?' This is a question of value, and its answer could only be a value statement. But this statement would be unverifiable: for it would require a higher set of criteria to verify it, and there cannot logically be a higher set of criteria than the ultimate set. Neither A nor B can offer any criteria to judge their ultimate criteria. They have run out of ammunition.

Our only hope, therefore, as we suggested in the last
section, is that they may be able in some way to share the
same set of criteria. There is no *logical* way of compelling
either of them to abandon his set, and adopt the other's,
as there is in the case of empirical statements. But there
may be other ways. This is not too hard to imagine, if we
remember that our adoption of an agreed meaning and
verification even for empirical statements depends ultimately on our common experience and desires. We can
logically compel someone to admit that what passes the
verification-tests for being 'red' is actually red: but we
cannot logically compel him to agree to accept the
verification-tests themselves. He usually does accept them,
because he has the same experiences and desires as other
men. In other words, there may be psychological reasons
why he should be a party to the agreement, even though
there are no logical reasons.

Even though we obviously do not always share the same
criteria or verification-tests for value statements, therefore,
there is hope that we may be able to do so. This hope is
augmented when we consider the numerous cases where
we do share them. We are agreed about the goodness of
things which are useful to us, such as knives, horses, motor-
cars, houses and many other things. We are also—and this
is perhaps more significant—agreed to a great extent about
the goodness of works of art, music and literature. Thus,
it is generally accepted, at least within European society,
that Beethoven and Bach are good composers, that
Shakespeare and Goethe are good writers, that Michel-
angelo and Velasquez are good painters. We share a
common set of criteria in judging their value.

We agree about such criteria of value as these for two
chief reasons—because we have had sufficient experience

and knowledge of the objects concerned, and because we are not usually subject to violent prejudices or emotional bias for or against them. This is particularly obvious in the judgments we make about works of art and literature. In order to reach agreement about these works, we require time to appreciate them and to learn about them, and the ability to consider their merit without prejudice or bias. That is why we are better able to agree about great artists who lived in the distant past than about modern artists: for with the latter, we have had insufficient time to experience their works, and are more subject to prejudice. The same is also true of our agreement about useful objects like knives and motor-cars. By knowing how they work, and not being prejudiced about them, we are able to agree which are to be called good and which bad. To put it briefly, we know what we *want* them to be like.

Where we do not share criteria, it is because either we do not yet possess enough factual knowledge, or we are prejudiced. This is sufficiently obvious if we consider the actual cases of disagreement about values. They nearly all concern the goodness or badness of *men*, and the actions, motives and political institutions of men. Even here, we are usually agreed on at least some points. Thus, we agree that taking another's legal property is bad, because it does not require very much experience for us to see that we do not want this kind of action. Even an observer who had no interest in supporting any kind of morality or religion would find it inconvenient to commend such behaviour. But where we disagree, we usually find both lack of knowledge and prejudice. Criteria of what counts as good sexual behaviour, for example, vary greatly from society to society and age to age. This is because very little is known of the results of different kinds of sexual behaviour on the people and society concerned; and also because people are liable to react strongly to any behaviour which does not accord with their own set of criteria. Hence few people are in a position to consider what criteria are the best without prejudice. Again, the value of one sort of society as against another—democracy versus totalitarianism, for instance—is not agreed, because few people ever have the experience of living under both systems, and few people are without prejudice.

We disagree about the criteria for human values, because we do not know much about human beings, and because we do not admit our ignorance, preferring prejudice instead. The sciences which are supposed to give us the information we require are, of course, psychology, sociology (which amounts to mass psychology), anthropology, and history. Of these sciences, none have yet reached the stage of advanced development where they can give unerring and useful information, and the first three are still in their infancy. Even so, they have already done much to bring the agreement on questions of value which we seek closer to us: psychology in particular has persuaded many people to change their criteria of value. As for our prejudice, we need only observe the way in which most people, even today, feel hostile towards these very sciences, and the strong and sometimes violent disapproval which those who believe themselves to be 'moral' display to those who hold other criteria.

The importance of science and the methods of science in this respect can hardly be overemphasised, for only a scientific approach to our problems of value can help to solve them. By 'a scientific approach' I mean, in the first place, that absence of prejudice and open-mindedness which characterises the work of a good scientist: and secondly, the operation of the scientific method of observation, experiment and hypothesis. Perhaps an example will help to make this clear. Until quite recently in our history the rightness of capital punishment for murder was almost universally accepted. It was considered right and just that a man who had killed should himself be killed. This seemed so obvious that nobody took the trouble to find out whether the death penalty acted as an effective deterrent to murder. It would have been wiser to doubt the obviousness of this principle at least to the extent of discovering the sociological results of the death penalty. A good scientist, I think, would have suspended judgment on the matter until he had been able to collect evidence by observation and experiment. Today many people are in serious doubt about the wisdom of capital punishment, and are well aware of the importance of the sociological sciences, particularly perhaps of statistics, in giving them enough facts to form a considered and un-prejudiced opinion. Such statistics as are available, for instance, do not by any means prove the contention that capital punishment is a uniquely effective deterrent; and this fact is plainly of great importance to anybody who wishes to judge the matter rightly.

The reason why the sociological sciences are still in their infancy is that most people, even today, find it abhorrent to adopt a scientific approach to problems which involve the behaviour – particularly the moral behaviour – of human beings. Thus in the not too distant past it was taken for granted that criminals should be treated harshly, that children should be brought up strictly and beaten when-ever they did not know their Latin grammar, and that certain types of sexual behaviour were dangerous and wicked. These are all things about which people have strong views, and towards which they adopt emotionally-conditioned attitudes. To allow scientists to investigate such matters seems to them unnecessary, for their minds are already made up; indeed, such investigation would represent a threat to their prejudices. Yet questions like 'What sort of treatment best reforms criminals, and what sort most effectively deters potential evildoers?', or 'What effect does prolonged physical punishment have on the minds of children?', are plainly important questions, and can only be answered by careful and patient scientific research. On the other hand, although the sociological sciences may still be weak, we owe their very existence partly to the great successes achieved by their elder brothers. It is partly because we have learned to rely upon the established sciences that we are today prepared, to some extent at least, to accept the use and importance of scientific method in dealing with human problems.

The advance of the relevant sciences must, of course, be left to the scientists concerned; and I shall say something about overcoming prejudice in a later section. Here we must note only that if we can gain the one, and conquer the other, we have every hope that our criteria will gradually come to be uniformly accepted throughout mankind. More knowledge and experience, on the one hand, of the things and people to which we assign or deny value, and less prejudice, on the other, will bring the agreement which we seek. Of course this cannot be proved: we shall have to wait and see, and in the meantime we must admit to doubt and ignorance. But since in all other cases where knowledge and lack of prejudice have been at work we have reached such agreement, it is very likely that this process will continue (or can continue) so as to cover cases in which we now disagree.

If that happens, we shall all hold the same set of criteria

for all values: and this is to say that we shall have agreed about the meaning and verification-method for all value statements. Then we shall be in a position to say what is true and what is not true in ethics with certainty: for our three conditions of truth (see section A of this chapter) will be able to be fulfilled. It will, of course, still be open to us to change our verification-method if we choose to do so: but that is not to the point. We can, and do, change our verification-method for empirical statements also. Provided that we all change together, we can still say what is true: for all that is necessary for discovering truth is that we should all be agreed about what method is appropriate.

D. METAPHYSICAL STATEMENTS

In the last chapter (section c, 5) we defined metaphysical statements as statements whose meaning and verification were not agreed. Our business here is to see if there is any method by which we might come to agree.

We must admit at once that many metaphysical statements, as we have already seen in the section quoted, must be classified as attitude-statements or value statements. In the former case the question of truth does not arise, for attitude-statements are not intended to convey truth; and in the latter, we can deal with them as we have already dealt with other value statements in the last section. What we are interested in is the type of metaphysical statement which we may be able to treat as conveying special information of its own: a type, therefore, analogous to empirical statements.

In considering value statements, we saw that lack of experience and the existence of prejudice had so far prevented us from reaching agreement about meaning and verification: and in section B, we saw that the basis for reaching such agreement in general depended on similarity of experience, and the usefulness of expressing it by means of established frameworks of verification. These considerations apply equally to metaphysical statements. Just as our sense-impressions allowed us to build up a framework of verification for empirical statements, and our common experiences and desires enabled us to agree about our verification of value statements, so it may be possible to discover or notice experiences of a special kind which we might use as a basis for the verification of metaphysical statements.

There seems to be no doubt that these special experiences do exist. There is certainly no logical reason to deny their possibility. We have already established the existence of different kinds of experience. When we use our senses, we have one sort of experience: when we consider whether we want to commend this action or that, we have another sort: when we consider whether a work of art is good or not, we have yet another sort: when we appreciate the nature of logical and mathematical rules, we have another sort again. For each of these types of experience, we have different frameworks of meaning and verification: hence the different types of statements described in the last chapter. Moreover, the facts seem to point to the existence of a special type of 'metaphysical' experience. That which is felt by religious people when they pray and worship, by mystics when they contemplate, or even by ordinary people when they feel 'in tune with' the world, seem all to be instances of a type of experience which exists in its own right, and cannot be assimilated to any other type.

It is not strictly necessary for the acceptance of a universal method of verification that all people should actually have these special experiences. Our experiences of art and music are very limited: we accept what critics and other experts tell us, because we believe that if we had time and inclination, we too should have the experiences they have. Similarly, we accept the findings of scientists, not through personal experience of their methods, but because we believe that we could make the same observations as they do, and would make the same deductions from them as they make. All that is necessary is that we should agree that these special experiences are available, that they are the same or similar for all or most people, and that we want to describe them in the same way. If we reach that agreement, we shall be able to agree about the use of verbal signs to describe them, and a common method of verification and meaning for statements about them.

What is needed, then, is an intensive investigation of these experiences. From that investigation it may emerge— I personally believe that it will—that there are at least some experiences which we may all have which we should want to describe by statements that are now classified as metaphysical. For example, if we all had experiences of what I shall loosely call 'love' and 'power' which could not be accounted for by observation of the natural world, we might wish to describe the source of these experiences by the word 'God'. 'God exists' would then have a definite meaning and method of verification, just as 'That table exists' has. By discovering these similar experiences, and agreeing to use certain signs to describe them, we should be able to build up a secure language of metaphysics. The statements of that language would not be metaphysical, in our sense of having doubtful meaning and verification. We might perhaps classify them all as 'empirical': or we might prefer to say that empirical statements were verified by sense-impressions and sense-experience, whereas these statements were verified by experience which was not given us by our senses. In the latter case we should have to find a new name for them, or else use 'metaphysical' in a different sense to the sense in which we have hitherto been using it.

Such investigation, however, has never been undertaken; and just as prejudice stands in the way of the social sciences, so it stands in the way of the investigation of religious or metaphysical experience on an objective basis. Most supporters of religion or any other type of metaphysical beliefs think that they already have the truth. In fact, of course, they cannot logically be in this position, since the three conditions of truth (see section A) have not been satisfied. But this does not prevent them from retaining their prejudice. I have dealt with this prejudice more fully in the next section.

I do not wish to commit myself on the question of which statements amongst those now classified as metaphysical will survive this investigation, and which will be found to be useless for purposes of truth and falsehood. I venture to believe that some, at least, can be removed from the 'metaphysical' class, and reclassified: that some, in other words, can be made to give genuine and true information, because people will agree to accept a definite meaning and verification for them. Others, as I have said, will remain metaphysical (and hence useless), or be absorbed into other statement-classes. But we must not allow prejudice either for or against any religion or metaphysic to prevent us from realising the true position. It cannot now be said with certainty of *any* metaphysical statement that it is true or false: it cannot even be said that it is meaningful or verifiable. But there is at least hope for the future.

E. PREJUDICE

The study of words, statements and language from a logical viewpoint is not merely an amusing game. Its purpose is to enlarge and clarify our knowledge and to discover truth: and this book will have failed if it does not enable its readers to do this more effectively. I have preferred throughout to appeal to reason, and not to use the persuasive tricks of honeyed words, skilful oratory, or emotional appeal to convince the reader. The latter would be self-stultifying: for it is part of my thesis that we have often to combat them as dangerous enemies. I have grouped them together under the title of 'prejudice': and we shall now see that it is perhaps this factor, more than any other, which stands between us and the truth.

For something to be true, we must remember, we have to be agreed about its meaning and its verification, and must have good evidence for it. One would have thought the importance of the first two of these conditions for attaining truth would have been sufficiently obvious to anyone at all interested in morals, politics or religion. But if they are obvious, at least no attempt is made to satisfy them. Moralists and ordinary people, governments and governed, clergy and laymen seem entirely unconcerned and unaware of the difficulties in giving their statements a definite meaning and method of verification. This looks very much like wilful ignorance, and does incalculable harm. Apparently it is not sufficient for our laws and educational system, to say nothing of uncontrolled propaganda, to impress upon adults and children the necessity of believing a large number of metaphysical and value statements, under pain either of social or religious disapproval, or physical punishment. Men are prepared to take more drastic action than that to enforce their unverifiable beliefs.

I need only quote two examples to show the damage that can be done by pretension to knowledge and truth, when even meaning and verifiability are not known. The mediaeval inquisitors tortured heretics and burnt them at the stake; and the Nazis in Germany, before and during the Second World War, persecuted and killed Jews. The alleged justification for these acts depended on statements which were entirely unverifiable, and possibly meaningless The inquisitors argued: 'By burning the bodies of these heretics, we shall save their souls: the soul is more important than the body: therefore we ought to burn their bodies'. The Nazis argued: 'Jews are not of Aryan blood: all those not of Aryan blood are inferior: we can do what we like with those who are inferior: therefore we can do what we like with Jews'. One should object to these arguments, not because the statements they contain are not true; for there might be genuine differences of opinion about that, and if they were true we could not object to the conclusions. We should object because they lack definite meaning and verification; and to torture and kill people on the basis of meaningless and unverifiable statements seems to border on insanity.

We have no time to investigate the causes for the widespread and occasionally fanatical opposition to discovering meaning and verification, for our business concerns the logic of statements, not the psychology of those who make and hear them. But a few observations may be useful. First, many people have a vested interest in preserving their metaphysical statements intact. The government of Russia, for example, has every reason to insist that all its citizens believe the doctrines which Communism enjoins; for if they do, they can be governed more easily. Most religions, also, fear that too much questioning—especially searching queries about meaning and verification—will prove their houses to have been built upon logical sand, and not on rock. Second, the social and moral behaviour of the majority of people is based on religious or other metaphysical premises, and whilst they may not feel strongly that the premises are true, they are afraid to question them lest the behaviour of others (particularly their children) should become immoral and antisocial. Thus, a parent may not himself believe in the divine origin and absolute authority of the Ten Commandments: but he may think it useful to try to get his children to believe in this, so that they shall not steal, lie, murder, and so on. Third, men's desire for knowledge is more apparent than real. Their basic desire is for security: and questioning necessarily involves the insecurity of doubt. For one has to doubt to some extent whether a statement is true in order to approach it with an open mind: if one is already certain, one would not approach it at all. Most people find it more snug and warm to keep their minds closed. When they argue and declare their beliefs, they do not do so with the scientific and rational desire for knowledge, but in order to persuade others and to increase their own sense of certainty and security. The difficulty of getting anyone who makes metaphysical statements to give them meaning and verification is sufficient evidence of this. Finally, statements whose meaning and verification are obscure usually express beliefs on matters which are very close to our hearts. They concern morals, politics, and religion: and all these are subjects about which most of us have strong views. We are only too liable to react emotionally to anyone who wishes to investigate them by the use of pure reason.

Many people are aware of their weakness in this respect

and try to cover it by supporting curious theories about truth and knowledge which attempt to evade the necessity for a rational investigation of meaning and verification altogether. Since these theories are supposedly logical, we ought perhaps to observe their more obvious weaknesses. They usually take the form of an attack upon reason: sometimes in the name of 'faith', sometimes in the name of 'intuition', sometimes in some other name. They also usually speak of 'truth' as if it were something which was not gained by thinking, but by some special faculty, usually of a mystic or magical nature: and they apply this view also to knowledge.

Our analysis of 'true' in the last part should suffice as an answer to all such theories. It is simply not sense to say that you know that something is true if you do not know what it means, or how to verify it. You may have as many and as exciting mystic or magical experiences as you like: you may be more saintly than the saints, more moral than the moralists, or more passionately concerned for political welfare than the politicians: but if you claim certain beliefs and statements to be true, then our three conditions of truth must be satisfied. Moreover, though this is really a side-issue, the process of reasoning is necessarily involved in satisfying them all. By 'reasoning' we mean simply the necessity of having 'reasons' or evidence for our beliefs. We may rely upon 'intuition', but we should not normally do so unless we had evidence that our intuitions were reliable: and the same argument applies to the acceptance of 'conscience', or any other human or divine authority, as a guide in life.

If we wish to deal in truth, knowledge and certainty at all, we cannot avoid the use of reason in the study of language. This does not abolish or diminish the importance of 'intuition', 'conscience', 'emotion', 'faith' or anything else. We need faith, but we need to have reasons for it. Thus we have faith in the engine-driver, because we have good evidence that he will bring us to our destination safely. If we wish to 'have faith in God', we must be able to produce reasons for it. We need emotion, but we need our reason to ensure that it is rightly used. We may place our trust in anything which we have reason to trust in. Of course, there are plenty of activities which are not concerned with truth or knowledge. If we are writing a poem, painting a picture, swimming, eating, sun-bathing and so forth, questions of truth or knowledge do not play a great part. But that lies outside our province.

Insofar as the activities of moralists. politicians, teachers, and men of religion are not concerned with the discovery and exposition of truth, but rather with exhortation, indoctrination, propaganda and poetic communication generally, it is not our business to quarrel with them. But insofar as they concern truth, we feel bound to make some suggestions which might help to overcome the present barriers to truth which we have just noted. We have seen that it is necessary to apply the study of language, and perhaps in particular of meaning and verification, to all doubtful statements which purport to be true. But we shall not be able to apply it effectively unless certain conditions are fulfilled.

1. We need freedom from governmental control. It is, and should be, the government's job to persuade its citizens to act in accordance with the principles of social and political behaviour which the majority think good, to encourage what it thinks to be virtue and prevent what it thinks to be vice, and in particular to prevent one individual or group from harming others. But if this entails,

as it need not, compelling its citizens to support unverifiable statements which are supposed to be true, by its
control of the law or the educational system, then the price
is nearly always too great. We may get a law-abiding and
uniformly stable society, but unless people are allowed to
challenge these metaphysical statements it will be a stag-
nant society and probably a dissatisfied one. Fortunately
the Western democracies have realised this vital point, unlike the totalitarian states. We are at least free from the
more obvious forms of governmental control. Yet much
still remains to be done. It can hardly be said that the
authorities as a whole encourage children and adults to
question the moral, political and religious beliefs of their
society. Admittedly, such questioning can be highly
dangerous, if it is not undertaken rationally; and it may be
justifiable under certain circumstances for governments to
prevent it. But without a good deal of questioning, we shall
not be able to discover truth: and without discovering
truth, there can be no real progress.

2. We need freedom from the control of religious and
public convention. The force of public opinion on religious
and moral questions can often be more compelling, and
can quash more attempts to discover truth, than the
direct control of any government. Again, we are fortunate
in this country, in that there is no single body of religious
or moral opinion that is overwhelmingly strong, and which
can make us conform to its beliefs almost by its mere
existence. This was true of the Church in the Middle Ages,
and is true of Communism in Russia today; and it has
usually been true of most societies. We ought to appreciate
our uniquely lucky position. Nevertheless, there are still
many people in our society whose opinions are shaped, not
by rational enquiry or teaching, but by what I can only

call the emotional shock-tactics of their immediate environment. At home and in school children are expected to hold certain metaphysical beliefs; and if they try to question them, they meet with the emotional disapproval of their elders. Perhaps this is to some extent inevitable; and it would not be dangerous, were it not that very few of these children ever get the chance of raising their doubts at a later stage. They mostly remain slaves to their environment: and under such circumstances one can hardly expect them to apply the study of language to beliefs which they have been forced to hold from an early age.

3. We need freedom from the control of our own emotions and fears. The two types of control mentioned above derive chiefly from the fear of doubt within the individual. We must recognise our own unwillingness to let go our hold upon cherished beliefs, even if they have hitherto formed the basis of our life, and take whatever steps we can to ensure that we do not pretend to knowledge that we do not possess. Most of our fears in this respect are empty ones. It is perfectly possible to lead a good life without giving assent to meaningless and unverifiable statements: indeed, it is difficult to see how giving assent to these statements can really benefit us at all. To recite a form of words which we do not understand may improve our self-confidence, but it can hardly improve our virtue. By all means let us indulge in poetic communication and ritualistic verbalism when we so desire: there are doubtless excellent psychological reasons why such indulgence should be desirable. But let us at least not base our lives upon ignorance.

Since this is not a book for politicians, moralists or clergymen only, but for ordinary people, we can suggest one remedy which might help us to overcome these barriers, and eventually to fulfil the above three conditions. It consists simply of getting as much practice as possible in applying the study of language to our beliefs. We can do this in the class-room, when we are thinking about our beliefs by ourselves, when we argue with others, read books, hear sermons and lectures, listen to speeches, and on all the thousand-and-one occasions when the truth of statements is in question. This is not difficult or specialist activity, to be labelled 'intellectual', 'highbrow', 'philosophical', and to be frightened of. It does not require outstanding intelligence: it requires only patience and the desire to learn. The results come with surprising speed. Let us at least try it, and see what happens.